Praise for *It's Not You, It's Everything*

"With *It's Not You, It's Everything*, Eric Minton gives us a profound gift, inviting us into a genuinely therapeutic space where we can regard our own, stretched-to-the-limit bandwidth with care, compassion, and good humor. He exemplifies this holy task by showing us that all justice is relational and that we ourselves did not create the infrastructures of toxic ideas about self, others, and God many of us have inherited. There is difficult work to be done, but we can meet the task of seeing ourselves clearly and candidly. It can even be a joy."

—David Dark, author of *Life's Too Short
to Pretend You're Not Religious*

"In *It's Not You, It's Everything*, Eric Minton presents a compassionate and uncompromising assessment of the forces driving our spiritual anxiety. Knitting together psychological and structural reasons for a culture engulfed in despair, Eric shows us how the dam of our discontent cannot be plastered over with therapeutic moments and marketplace distractions. It will take stronger stuff to pull apart the blockage of our personal and communal destruction. *It's Not You, It's Everything* guides us toward questions that peel back the source of our discontent. In this book for people who can't take much more, Minton offers us a hope with weight—hope we can hold on to."

—Melissa Florer-Bixler, pastor and author of
How to Have an Enemy and *Fire by Night*

"In *It's Not You, It's Everything*, you will find an honest, congenial, and instructive book. Eric Minton is vulnerable, sharing both his mental health journey and his reckoning with the faulty folk religion of his youth: white evangelical American Christianity and the ecosystem that keeps it obscured and impervious to remedy. Then, through his stories and keen insights, he shows us a way forward."

—Lisa Colón DeLay, spiritual director, author of *The Wild
Land Within*, and host of the *Spark My Muse* podcast

It's Not You, It's Everything

It's Not You, It's Everything

What Our Pain
Reveals about the
Anxious Pursuit of
the Good Life

Eric Minton

Broadleaf Books
Minneapolis

IT'S NOT YOU, IT'S EVERYTHING
What Our Pain Reveals about the Anxious Pursuit of the Good Life

Some names, details, and identities have been changed or significantly obscured to protect individuals' privacy.

Cover image: Stacey__M/shutterstock
Cover design: Olga Grlic

Print ISBN: 978-1-5064-7191-4
eBook ISBN: 978-1-5064-7192-1

Printed in Canada

Contents

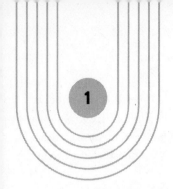

How (Not) to Float

> There is nothing more difficult to outgrow than anxieties that have become useful to us, whether as explanations for a life that never quite finds its true force or direction, or as fuel for ambition, or as a kind of reflexive secular religion that, paradoxically, unites us with others in a shared sense of complete isolation: you feel at home in the world only by never feeling at home in the world.
>
> —Christian Wiman, *My Bright Abyss*

"That mother&*@%er stole my brand, and I swear to God I'm fixing to go off on his ass if he tries to get on Facebook Live with my shit" is how a teenager angrily addressed me a few years ago. This was after he was forcibly recused from math class at the underfunded high school where I once worked as a psychotherapist. If you are unfamiliar with the way language works for some of our youngest citizens and don't comprehend what that first sentence means, please utilize the same skills you employ at contentious Thanksgiving dinner conversations and during episodes of *The Bachelor* and simply pay attention to the pain, because the pain is trying to tell us something.

In this case, the pain could be better understood as the extreme *angst* of a student who has had a peer "steal" his "brand" (way of being, style of humor, mode of speech) and go live on the internet as if it were the aforementioned thief's own brand. While I may not remember everything about my fumbling travails through adolescence in the early aughts, I am fairly certain that copyright infringement wasn't yet part of the landscape of my own acne-filled and hormone-fueled existence. I do, however, recognize the pain.

In the face of teenage meltdowns, it can be easy for us adults to find ourselves muttering something unhelpful about the good old days, that things will probably get better and that angst is what adolescence is and has always been about since modern economic theory began categorizing these almost-adults as their own consumer bloc in the early 1900s. However, before dismissing them to bed without dinner *because you will not speak to your mother that way*, I would argue that teenagers are telling—strike that, *yelling* at—us the uncomfortable truth about who we are as a nation, what we believe in, and what we value most in this world.

Whenever we find ourselves offended or confused by adolescent behavior, it isn't just the behavior itself we find offensive but rather the ways in which the anxious, performative, technology-addled, and sometimes narcissistic or status-driven lives of our teenagers say the quiet part of being an American out loud. And the truth isn't pretty. I'm saying that all this aired pain might actually be expressing the truth about what it feels like to try to survive in America right now. So instead of talking them out of their tantrums, maybe we should instead start listening to our teenagers because they might be right to be upset.

I'M NOT OKAY; YOU'RE NOT OKAY

Over the last twenty years, most of my work as a pastor and now therapist has been with teenagers and their families. From majority white, middle- and upper-middle-class churches and Christian summer camps to small college campuses and underfunded high schools with incredibly diverse populations, the teenagers I meet have one thing in common: an almost cellular uneasiness in the world. What I love most about these teenagers—especially ones regularly referred to as "emotionally disturbed," "problems," or "one of *those* kids"—is their ability to colorfully lay bare the aspirations, fears, values, and stinging contradictions of the systems they are attempting to survive. Teenagers are unapologetically themselves, even if they aren't always sure who they are just yet.

This simple fact led some of the early thinkers of the systems-driven family therapy movement to treat everything interrupting typical adolescent development—from schizophrenia to eating disorders—as less the result of individual pathology and more the cries of an entire family, community, and society in pain. According to these philosophers, researchers, and psychotherapists, the "problem kids" aren't broken or crazy. Instead, they're the only ones telling the truth about what actually runs our world.

The difficulty in receiving teenagers' sometimes gruff witness arises whenever we adults confuse the medium for the message, the tone for the content. Becoming a therapist to adolescents has given me the unexpected gift of sitting across from another human who has yet to be stooped by the regular complications, occupational stresses, and crippling knee pain of adulthood. Even the word *adulthood* itself serves as a colloquialism for a sort of existential cocktail of missed opportunities and mortality all of us are expected to live with as an act of self-disciplined resignation. Amid their quaking rage and expert eye rolls, teenagers—yes, even teenagers of color who have themselves already been rapidly aged by white supremacy—maintain this unrelenting, prophetic belief in a world whose awfulness isn't briefly interrupted by commercial breaks for a pill that reduces the unwanted side effects of our antidepressants. Or, as one colleague put it to me early in my therapeutic career, teenagers are our symptoms incarnate. Their angst represents a collective, embodied frustration at the state of our world because *teenagers are our own pain made flesh.*

In a study from the year 2000, psychologist Dr. Jean Twenge performed a meta-analysis of anxiety in schoolchildren and college students in order to track the development of anxiety and depression generation to generation. She found that more than forty years ago in

1980, "typical schoolchildren" reported more anxiety than did child psychiatric patients in the 1950s. This finding led Dr. Twenge, prophetically, to posit that "the results of the study suggest that cases of depression will continue to increase in the coming decades, as anxiety tends to predispose people to depression."

Some twenty years after her study, amid sound bite after sound bite elucidating the grisly details of the medicated, anxious, suicidal, and depressed world our young people are inhabiting, it can be easy to find ourselves heaving and buried under the weight of what we have done to them. The National Institutes of Health recently reported that nearly one in three adolescents aged thirteen to eighteen will experience an anxiety disorder, and according to the Centers for Disease Control and Prevention, suicide is the second leading cause of death in American youth ages ten to twenty-four. This represents, disturbingly, a tripling of the suicide rate in this population from 2007 to 2017.

The kids are, clearly, not all right.

HOW (NOT) TO FLOAT

But I'm getting ahead of myself. So first things first: my name is Eric, and I'm a terrible swimmer. My wife reminds me of this every summer when she briefly offers to teach me to tread water. "Eric, you have to relax your body!" is something she typically shouts at me any time my arm and leg motions take on the desperate characteristics of one of those flailing inflatable tubepeople outside a used car dealership. And yes, if you were wondering, an almost-translucent adult man wearing a sun shirt and trying to keep his head above water in the deep end of a crowded hotel pool is exactly as cool as it sounds. I want to be clear, though: my problems in the water stem not from a refusal to put in enough effort—that's never been the issue—but from trying too hard to force the water to hold me up.

You see, I never learned to swim properly as a kid. Because of this, I don't actually trust my ability to survive in the water without putting in what feels like a Herculean amount of effort. My wife's request, then—to believe that I only become more buoyant, safer even, when I cease my anxious efforts at staying afloat—sounds not only stupid but suicidal. So each summer my survivalist impulse gets the better of me, and I begin flailing faster and faster and faster, forgetting that the same thing always ends up dragging me down. I like to think this happens not because I'm an idiot but because I am afraid of sinking. This misplaced and misapplied self-interested fear effectively drowns out every well-intentioned shout from the pool deck to relax my body and let the water do its job.

There are very real reasons I, an adult in his late thirties, can't swim effectively. Some of them have to do with a fundamental lack of technique or skill, but most stem from the simple fact that from my earliest days on earth, no one ever taught me how to float: how to trust and how to exist in a world where drowning is always possible, but so is buoyancy. I came of age under the watchful eyes of a God I could never please, a family I uneasily fit within, and a world where I often felt misunderstood and alone. I endeavored to fix my problems by anxiously performing my way into being loved, known, and whole. I grew up believing that if I worked hard enough, one day I might start enjoying life rather than just trying to survive it. I even became a Baptist pastor to try to fix what had been broken not only within me but within all of us. I'm here to tell you, dear reader, *it didn't work.*

Eventually, as my arms grew weary from struggling to stay afloat, I began feeling worthless to the disappointed God I grew up with, to our broken world, to my wife, and even to my own newborn son, blinking up at me after my long shift at the grocery store where I worked after quitting my job as a pastor. Despite my best efforts, I started sinking, hoping to drown, because at least then there might be insurance money my family could use to pay the mortgage. It was here, at the ragged edge of a life filled with "so much potential," when I found myself most wanting to die, to drown, that I was too exhausted to do anything but finally let the water hold me up. And the strangest thing happened: it *did.*

Several years later I am finding—as a now former Baptist pastor turned psychotherapist—that the thing often keeping my patients from swimming effectively is the same thing that made it hard for me. While some of their issues may have to do with a fundamental lack of technique or skill, most stem from the simple fact that from *their* earliest days on earth, no one ever taught them how to float: how to trust and how to exist in a world where drowning is always possible, but so is buoyancy. I would argue that no one ever showed you, or me, or any of us how to be okay because they worried that a lack of effort, anxious energy, or hard work would be the thing that ultimately killed us, bankrupted us, or derailed our futures. When, in fact, the opposite is true.

Our country's commitment to bottomless self-interest, manic work schedules, and a structural belief in competition and scarcity as moral imperatives is *actually* killing us. "Most of us were not taught how to recognize pain, name it, and be with it," Brené Brown argues. "Our families and culture believed that the vulnerability that it takes to acknowledge pain was weakness, so we were taught anger, rage and denial instead. But what we know now is that when we deny our emotion, it owns us."

Whenever I hear words like *depression* and *anxiety* come out of the mouths of my patients, I immediately wonder, What are you taking responsibility for that isn't yours to bear? What is not working about the world around you? What problem are you embodying for the sake of other people, families, and whole communities? Like our angry teenagers, what pain have you been quietly (or loudly in front of company) bearing that was never meant to be yours alone?

Yet while depression and anxiety are great at noticing what *isn't* working, they are terrible at fixing it. This is primarily because our culture has taught us to interpret the presence of these feelings as a form of internalized failure. When, in fact, much of our pain actually stems from forces larger than our ability to work harder and smile more. It isn't just you who can't stay afloat in these waters; it's all of us. So maybe instead of ignoring, grinding through, or desperately rebranding our pain as some sort of necessary accelerant to living a productive, meaningful, and eventually restful life, what if we just listened to it for a moment? Because I want to argue that the problem isn't just our troubled kids but their context. That it isn't just our misfiring brains but our culture. That it's not just you; it's *everything*.

THE PAIN IS A MIRROR

Rather than fixating on the way our adolescents dress and talk—not to mention their paradoxical willingness to use a phone for anything but its original purpose—in this book we will first pay attention to their pain because their pain is a mirror. Malcolm Harris aptly describes the asphyxiating quality of modern American childhood in his book *Kids These Days*: "A hypercompetitive environment sets parents up for dreams of champion children, and then for almost inevitable heartbreak. Millennials of all abilities have grown up in the shadow of these expectations, expectations that by definition only a very few of us can fulfill."

Adolescents across the socioeconomic spectrum possess a nascent understanding of the weight of disappointment and expectation they regularly toil underneath. It's why they have (and are) "brands" and why they graduate with GPAs nearing six on a four-point scale. It's why they have life plans at age twelve and talk about the economic outlook for employment in the pharmaceutical field. But it's not just them; it's all of us. *Their* overextended, stressed, and desperate childhood is our adulthood.

Consider the ways those of us in early or middle adulthood conceive of our own ability to retire, or pay the rent, or cultivate a lifestyle brand on Instagram, or obtain health insurance, or offer our children a global perspective through travel, or find someone to watch them when we pull a double, or pay off our crippling student loan debt, or afford to own a home whose kitchen can eventually be painted white and wrapped in shiplap. *It's exhausting.* Or think of the ways those of us in later adulthood conceive of our ability to retire or continue being retired, or ethically consume the news on Facebook, or keep up with the labyrinthine demands of state-funded and private health insurance payment plans, or make end-of-life decisions for aging parents, or raise grandchildren whose parents have been consumed by opioids and a hyperventilating economic system, or ask questions at night about what kind of life we have lived and passed on to others.

It isn't just the teens who're anxious and depressed. It's just that they have the good sense to stop pretending that this kind of pain is normal.

BUT WHAT IF WE *WERE* OKAY?

Many Americans have been taught since birth that life is about owning or being owned by the world rather than loving or being loved by the world. This kind of life can only produce what psychologists, psychiatrists, and researchers feel comfortable calling "the most stressed people in the world." This book asks a rather simple question in a moment in which there are any number of more complex psychological, economic, political, and pharmacological responses to the chest-tightening atmosphere of being alive right now—that is, *What if we were okay?*

To be clear, I don't mean "okay" in the trite, lobotomized way it's often employed by the powerful and privileged in the face of a necessary outpouring of unrest and collective rage. I'm not trying to silence your pain the way your family did whenever they changed the subject to keep the peace at dinner. I'm doing the opposite. I want you to listen to your pain—to slow down in its presence and respect its perspective—because it isn't wrong to be upset, depressed, or incredibly anxious right now. "Depression embodies the final dissent of soul," psychologist Bruce Rogers-Vaughn claims. "It constitutes, as it were, the last outpost of the autoimmune system of soul. It is the visceral, organismic response of soul to a world no longer fit for human habitation. It is, in effect, the final cry of soul just this side of extinction."

In *Remember This House*, an unfinished thirty-page manuscript on the lives and assassinations of Malcolm X, Medgar Evers, and Martin Luther King Jr., James Baldwin reminds us that "not everything that is faced can be changed, but nothing can be changed until it is faced." We aren't wrong to be in pain. Our anxious teenagers know it, our hyper-ventilating free market knows it, our angry social media feeds know it, our polarized democracy knows it, and our dying planet knows it. Even our own bodies know it. I want to argue that all of this pain has a source—that of a thoroughly internalized capitalism—which can be broadly characterized as an economic system turned personal philosophy that constantly undermines our collective action against it through capital-protecting law-and-order policies as well as crip-plingly unequal access to resources, education, health care, and other social services. Internalized capitalism even seeks to invalidate our own inner revolt at what we see happening to ourselves, our children, and the world around us.

There are very real reasons that "normal life" is currently defined as checking email in the middle of the night, investing thousands in our child's travel soccer team, witnessing police brutality on our smart-phones over lunch, and becoming regularly enraged at high school classmates on Facebook. It's time we stopped asking questions about why we aren't more productive, successful, or okay with this kind of life and started asking how the hell this kind of life became normal in the first place.

I believe that as we finally begin facing the truth of a world where our pain has frequently been maintained, stoked, and operationalized for the flourishing of an insatiable free market, our radical okayness becomes something more than mere "self-care." Being okay is instead a form of political and spiritual resistance that gives us enough space and freedom to consider the creative possibilities of a world beyond competition, scarcity, and self-interest. Radical okayness is a Sabbath interruption of the morality of frenetic productivity that has co-opted our selfhood, smartphones, spirituality, and sanity. Radical okayness might sound suicidally passive because it is. But that's how floating feels to brands pretending to be humans and humans pretending to be brands.

For the past thirty-seven years, I have struggled to face the truth that no matter how hard I press, my desperate self-interest won't ever save me. It only exhausts me, angers me, alienates me from people who love me or wish to help me, makes me heavier, and eventually causes me to sink. As my wife is patiently teaching me, to float—to be truly okay—is to have a kind of radical trust that the water will hold me up whenever I finally cease fighting it or forcing it to. *Because that's its job.*

In the wake of my sudden buoyancy, the job I've now been given is to do something a bit more interesting than just anxiously surviving the world. Jesus once called this sort of life one founded on a self-sacrificing form of "love," and I've always been rather fond of that. This is a book about learning to float, to trust, and to love, even if it sometimes feels like you might drown in the process. Which is another way of saying that in a society ruled by a violent and religiously maintained self-interest pretending to be gospel truth, perhaps both death and resurrection are in order.

But to talk about that, we first need to talk about my pain, your pain, and what has always been "our" pain. We'll start with what has happened to "the kids," and your smartphone, and the economy, and my inherited Christian tradition. This investigation will help us track this pain, listen to it, and eventually, let it transform us and everything else.

Let's get started.

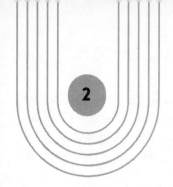

Why Is Kindergarten the New First Grade?

How Children Became Investments

From our bathroom breaks to our sleep schedules to our emotional availability, Millennials are growing up highly attuned to the needs of capital markets. We are encouraged to strategize and scheme to find places, times, and roles where we can be effectively put to work. Efficiency is our existential purpose, and we are a generation of finely honed tools, crafted from embryos to be lean, mean production machines.

—Malcolm Harris, *Kids These Days*

I used to be a professional Christian. Since my midtwenties, upon finishing seminary and being ordained by my childhood Baptist church in East Tennessee, I have frequently been paid to pray. Professionally, my business card read "youth pastor." Depending on what part of the world you're from, where you went to high school, and just how many friends you had praying for you, the title of youth pastor may conjure visions of a goateed gatekeeper to a promised land filled with endless games of laser tag, broken foosball tables, the phrase "doing life," and sodas your mom never let you drink past seven thirty on a school night. Or as seventh-grade Jean-Paul Sartre would have put it had you invited him to the lock-in down at the local Lutheran church, "Hell is other people sharing a communal bowl of Chex Mix at three thirty in the morning. *Dodgeball!*"

Normally, in the Baptist world at least, freshly minted reverends (regardless of fit) often find themselves suddenly charged with providing not only pastoral care for seventh to twelfth graders but also a rich social and activity calendar that meets their ever-changing needs and desires. "Jesus, but with water balloons" is how one senior clergyperson once described my job to a group of parishioners. Except that when I started working with adolescents in faith-based settings, they were increasingly unavailable to throw water balloons, play laser tag, or come to youth group meetings because things like out-of-town soccer tournaments, violin camp, or extra ACT prep kept getting in the way. When they *were* able to show up, some had a hard time staying seated, awake, or off their phones because they were anxiously refreshing their school's online grade book, experiencing the "come down" off of their meds, or barely keeping their eyes open after pulling an all-nighter the day before. I still remember a small group meeting in which a twelve-year-old admitted he had cried during a school assembly at his high-achieving middle school earlier that day. "They wanted all of us to come up with a life plan from now to adulthood—school, job, kids, house, all of it—and I couldn't think of anything," he said. "I just froze, and I felt like without a future, I'm gonna be a total failure."

It didn't seem like a good time to hit him with a water balloon.

IT'S THE END OF THE WORLD, AND
I HAVE A TEST IN THE MORNING

"All of a sudden I couldn't do anything. I was so afraid. You know how a normal person might have their stomach lurch if they walk into a classroom and there's a pop quiz? Well, I basically started having that feeling all the time." These are the words of a high school senior, Jake from North Carolina, in a piece for the *New York Times* in late 2017 entitled "Why Are More Teenagers Than Ever Suffering from Extreme Anxiety?" One of the more confusing components of Jake's description of the increasing intensity of his anxiety—an anxiety that left him incapacitated and unwilling to attend school in the latter part of his junior year despite being an honor student—is the *suddenness* of it all.

For Jake, a certain degree of resting anxiety was an expected by-product of caring about one's future: "The relentless drive to avoid such a fate seemed to come from deep inside [Jake]. He considered it a strength." The problem arises whenever this "relentless drive" leaves our teenagers unable to get out of bed. It's almost as if no one ever told Jake that living this way isn't worth it and that anxiety eventually does that to all of us. It's almost as if everyone was more afraid of Jake becoming a failure than they were of him being miserable.

Three years later, another major American news outlet, the *Washington Post*, quoted eighteen-year-old Sarah Niles's summation of the compounding quality of teenage anxiety in America, one characterized by the degradation of our environment, the possibility of a renewed global pandemic, active-shooter drills, economic instability, and the increasingly high stakes of high school: "It's like, the ice caps are melting and my hypothetical children will never see them, but also I have a calculus test tomorrow."

The world is probably ending, but maybe not yet, so in the meantime, I really should beef up my extracurriculars if I want to be competitive during early admission season—is there a more apt summation for American teenagerdom right now than this?

Troubling in all this coverage of American teenagers' crumbling mental health is both the occasional and terrifying spike in panic attacks and acute expressions of self-harm and suicidal ideation as well as the more insidious ways in which American children now utilize anxiety as a sort of accelerant to produce the kind of work they need to in order to avoid becoming failures. At first blush, experiences like those of Jake, Sarah, and the other high achievers in my old youth group might seem like statistical outliers. As the logic so often goes, these anxious teens merely represent the anxious fruit of an anxious childhood defined by unchecked social media use, rampant over-scheduling, needless affluence, and parental expectations run amok.

Images of ailing suburban white kids, buckling under the weight of an entire cul-de-sac's hopes and dreams, make it terribly easy to victim blame. It seems these days as if there is an ever-growing number of kids whose increased access to abundant resources and experiences has only produced a mass of humans devoid of the same fortitude, resilience, and coping skills many of us believe were forged in the fires of our own much more difficult childhoods. You can almost hear our nation's parents angrily ranting at their children on the other side of locked bedroom doors: "And if you think *my* mother would have spent $300 a week on ACT test prep, you're even crazier than your life coach accuses you of being!"

The problem with this extremely popular (not to mention cathartic) explanation for why many American teenagers are all suddenly just a cycle of screen-based malaise and mania-fueled production is that it fails to account for a simple truism about parenting: no child comes out of the womb spoiled, or abused, or a Detroit Lions fan. These things are taught, implicitly and explicitly. Our collective generational anger may feel righteously indignant as it comes screaming out of us at Target whenever our fifteen-year-old cusses us out because we refused to upgrade her phone. But it isn't helpful. This is because what raised these kids and what motivates our own anger and desperation as their parents now refuses to be tidily summed up by some tired trope about "kids these days." It's way worse than that.

Even if you don't have kids, we must begin facing the fact that *all of us* are attempting to carve out lives in an age of market-driven scarcity, violence, and collective anxiety motivated by our own fears of failure and an increasingly narrowing window of opportunity for ourselves and our children. We are very afraid, and the kids can smell it on us. As one teenager put it to me early in my pastoral career, "It's the strangest feeling to be abandoned by parents who are always around, coaching you, checking your homework, saving for college, but never really *there*. I felt like I lost my parents when I hit middle school."

The depression, anxiety, self-harm, and suicidal ideation pouring out of our country's youngest citizens are not just pressing medical or mental health problems to be addressed. At a deeper level, this experience is a collective pain to be empathized with and a warning to be heeded: the desperation many of us have become accustomed to drowning out with compulsive work, boxed wine, Instagram scrolls, and bottomless trips to Costco is slowly killing everyone, but *it's coming for the kids first.* Parents may have once believed they could mitigate the impact or hide this undercurrent of fear—baked into us by a heaving market economy—from their children by nervously giving them more of everything. But the damn thing ended up leaking out all over them anyway. Glennon Doyle perfectly encapsulates the desperation that is modern parenting in *Untamed*: "We obsess over our children's snacks while they rehearse their own deaths in active-shooter drills at school. We agonize over their college prep while the earth melts around them. I cannot imagine that there has ever been a more overparented and underprotected generation."

THE ANXIETY IS TRYING TO HELP US

Despite how all this anxiety may be depicted popularly—in articles, blogs, and best sellers highlighting the helicoptering work of middle- to upper-middle-class moms and dads—researchers are discovering that for teenagers writ large, anxiety and depression outpace all other concerns by a relatively wide margin. This is true across demographic groupings like ethnicity and socioeconomic status. If you think this system is bad for kids with tennis elbow, imagine coming of age in a world characterized by institutional abandonment, addiction, police brutality, a crumbling educational infrastructure, and the realization that as a teenager of color, you have already been left behind. As one fourteen-year-old Black student put it to me during my first month on the job at her high school, "Man, I was f&%$ed *long* before I got here." When these findings are set in context with a doubling in hospitalizations for self-harm and suicidal ideation over the last ten years in all children ages five through seventeen—with particularly large spikes in hospital admissions during the spring and fall school semesters—we have what amounts to a national emergency.

In the acuity of our present moment, one where every decision about child-rearing—from organic yogurt brands to private violin lessons—is fraught, it is nearly impossible for the adults in the room to get a hold of themselves. And all of this not-okayness on the part of adults actually compounds the problem. It motivates shortsighted educational policy decisions, and it redirects our country's meager mental health resources toward symptom alleviation and industries almost solely committed to getting adolescents back to work as quickly as possible in order to minimize the impact of all this on something we keep calling "their future." These kinds of institutional responses to the pain of "our kids" shift the conversation from who American children *are* to what they can do and how much they will one day earn.

Whenever we as adults focus on reducing the impact of these acute expressions of anxiety and depression on the long-term productivity of adolescents—through the administration of more psychotropic medication than any country on earth, for instance—we fail to ask questions about what kind of world produces so many anxious kids in the first place. To be fair, I regularly find that medication provides my patients with enough support—much like bowling alley bumpers that keep balls in the middle of the lane—to explore what drives much of their distress without that distress physically overwhelming them. To expect medication to accomplish this kind of work alone, though, is a tough ask. After all, the pain and the anxiety are there for a reason.

Regardless of what you may have heard, anxiety is actually an incredibly helpful component of human life, one that has kept us alive for millennia. Anxiety is why we break into a cold sweat and a light jog when a twig snaps in the woods behind us or why the thought of eating Taco Bell after midnight in our midthirties preemptively causes our stomachs to lurch; it's trying to help us! Ignoring environmental factors that lead our young people to respond to every test, quiz, and missed assignment like it will be their last fails to honor the far more terrifying truth at the bottom of all this: maybe our teenagers aren't wrong to be afraid of the world we have created. Maybe our kids are simply incarnating the bald truth of what it means to grow up in a winner-take-all society teaching us from birth to view childhood, according to Malcolm Harris, as "no longer a time to make mistakes; now it's when bad choices have the biggest impact." Maybe it's actually easier if our kids have an anxiety or depression problem. Frankly, maybe it's easier if our kids *are* the problem than it is to consider the possibility that something bigger is at play—something that affects all of us, even if we refuse or are unable to see it.

WE ARE WHO *THEY* ARE

In his book *Strangers to Ourselves*, University of Virginia psychologist Timothy Wilson notes that humans process roughly 11 million pieces of information per second during a given day. Due to the sheer volume of input, our brains are forced to limit the amount of data to which they give conscious thought and attention. "The most liberal estimate is that people can process consciously about 40 pieces of information per second," Wilson writes. The other 10,999,960 data points, he argues, are left to the supervision of our subconscious, shaped by years of evolution, herd survivalism, genetics, environmental influences, and episodes of *Judge Judy* watched in the waiting rooms of our country's auto repair and health care industries. Wilson quips that when Freud first popularized the idea of the conscious mind as the tip of a mental iceberg in humans, "he was short of the mark by quite a bit—it may be more the size of a snowball on top of that iceberg."

The most counterintuitive aspect of Wilson's research is that further self-introspection—navel-gazing, if you will—does not often bring about a great deal more congruency between our implicit and explicit values, directives, and decisions. The regular incongruity between the stories we tell ourselves about who we are and the concrete actions we engage in is a completely normal phenomenon. Our self-conceptions and self-understandings are notoriously biased and present overly favorable pictures of who we think we are, even when our actions in the world might beg to differ. "It can thus be fruitless to try to examine the adaptive unconscious by looking inward," Wilson notes. "It is often better to *deduce* the nature of our hidden minds by looking outward at our behavior and how others react to us, and coming up with a good narrative." Eschewing popular wisdom from Mom and Dad, Wilson encourages us to begin seeing ourselves *as others see us*, assiduously tracking and studying our behaviors as if they were the behaviors of someone else. This practice provides an incredibly helpful window into who we are, considering so much of our life is lived on autopilot.

I want to take Wilson's work a step further as it concerns the precipitous rise in the relative not-okayness of our nation's young people. When we begin seeing others as ourselves, like Jesus once put it, paying close attention to their movements, decision-making, and emotionality, we are given reams of raw data into who *all of us* are, societally, when no one is looking—including ourselves. More so, if these "others" are our own children—the teenagers sulking upstairs, for instance—it provides a certain clarity and ready responsibility to ask hard questions about what kind of values we have communicated and what kind of world we have created for our kids.

Some of these questions might sound like this: How exactly did we get to a place where 7.5 million adolescents are regularly taking psychotropic medication? Or why do we encourage "gifted" seventh graders to sit for the ACT? Or why do some baseball-playing ten-year-olds have private pitching coaches and Instagram brands? Or why has popular educational policy transformed kindergarten into "the new first grade"? Or why, after all these years spent paying lip service to boot-strapping American ingenuity, is the strongest predictor of physical and financial well-being in adulthood still (according to Harvard sociologist Robert Putnam) the unholy trinity of family income, social capital, and parental education levels?

Our kids intrinsically know this, and it's past time we became conscious of the ways our children have passively imbibed and later incarnated the noxious fumes of our nationwide commitment to scarcity and competition as economic, educational, and family policy. What is happening to our children is happening to us. The startling, inchoate, and sometimes violent lack of okayness we abhor in them is our own. To better understand our own pain, we have to look both at what we've been doing to ourselves as Americans and at what we see happening to our children. For starters, maybe we should ask why we have been "investing" so aggressively in the kids in the first place.

BOOTSTRAPS AND BOTTLENECKS

In 2015, the USDA reported that the average cost of raising a child in America amounted to roughly a quarter of a million dollars. This figure does not include the cost of postsecondary education, which in 2015 was estimated at an additional $43,370 and $20,090 per year for private and public institutions, respectively. So the total price tag for keeping a single American child housed, clothed, fed, watered, and publicly educated appears to be an eye-popping $330,000. These numbers, of course, represent an exponential rise in childhood investment since at least the early 1970s. Yet these numbers fail to account for the fact that income inequality is now, according to economist Thomas Piketty, higher than at any time since the Great Depression. It would follow that as incomes have ballooned for the top 10 percent of American households (even during the economic downturns of 2008 and 2020) while remaining relatively flat for middle-class, working-class, and impoverished families, so has childhood enrichment spending. Emory University sociologist Dr. Sabino Kornich argues that this ever-widening spending gap separating the children of affluent families from those living in poverty helps to explain the relative ineffectiveness of improved educational opportunities to close the gaps between later achievement scores in wealthy and impoverished students.

When this increasingly unequal childhood spending is coupled with the impact of our country's long-standing commitment to systemic racism and the near-wholesale abandonment of institutional safety nets for families and children across our nation, there appears to be no future for any of our kids, no matter our zip codes, tax brackets, or tireless efforts at getting our kids into *that* elementary school. Robert Putnam concludes as much in *Our Kids*, his inquiry into the inequalities facing modern American children. "Without succumbing to political nightmares, we might ponder whether the bleak, socially estranged future facing poor kids in America today could have unanticipated political consequences tomorrow," he writes. "So quite apart from the danger that the opportunity gap poses to American prosperity, it also undermines our democracy and perhaps even our political stability."

Our country's ever-rising income inequality not only works to effectively undermine social mobility and wide-reaching educational opportunities but also creates an environment of scarcity. An environment where a stubborn belief in meritocracy leads many of us Americans, unquestioningly, to sacrifice the futures of our own and others' children on the altar of an ever-evaporating bottleneck of "opportunity." The hyperventilating free market, it would seem, has begun raising, educating, and shaping American children from their earliest moments on earth. Many of us entered the world creating debt and anxiety for our parents, which can't help but trickle down to us and the kids we're now raising ourselves. If you don't believe me, you haven't spent much time on the nervous bleachers, ball fields, and basketball courts dotting our country's landscape.

"IT ALL JUST KEEPS GOING UP AFTER THAT"

A friend once confessed to me the cost for his teenage son to play competitive baseball, excluding weekend travel and hotel accommodations. "I mean, it makes me uncomfortable to even say it out loud, but we're talking at least three grand just to get started with uniforms, enrollment, tournament registrations, stuff like that," he told me. "And it all just keeps going up after that." A 2017 *Time* cover story on the American childhood sports industrial complex echoed my friend's plight, as it tracked the rapid transformation of a once quaint rite of passage for American boys and girls into a $15 billion a year industry—one featuring $100-an-hour pitching coaches, endorsement deals for ten-year-old basketball players, and parents willing to shell out "10% of their income on registration fees, travel, camps and equipment."

One confusing component behind the ballooning budgets of American kids' sports is the steepening decline of actual children participating in them. In 2018, the *Atlantic* found that only 34 percent of children from families earning less than $25,000 played a team sport at least one day in 2017, compared to 69 percent of children from households making more than $100,000. As a way of comparison, in 2011 these numbers were 42 and 66 percent, respectively.

All of this time, energy, and money spent on competitive youth sports and alternative childhood enrichment activities—fueled by the increasing paucity of coveted scholarships, internships, and future employment opportunities—lays bare the bedrock truth of parenting in a fundamentally unequal society: invest early, invest often, and invest *everything*. In this kind of environment, Malcolm Harris argues that phrases like "think of your kid" are subversively translated into "be afraid" or "buy this or else," resulting in what he calls "good advice for maximizing an individual kid's chance at success in a winner-take-all market, but we can see what kind of society—and person—results."

Despite what we may expressly believe about the parental ethics of such behavior, it is this implicit, often unconscious messaging that ends up directly shaping most of what we do to and for our children. Sports psychologist Jim Taylor grimly noted his own parental tension for *Time*: "It's hard not to get sucked in. Even for someone like myself, a quote-unquote expert on this stuff. Because I'm human. I'm a dad." From the $70 million "Sports Campus" that has almost singlehandedly resurrected the local economy of Westfield, Indiana, to the thriving test-prep and college acceptance consulting industries that exist like barnacles on the side of our children's educational infrastructure, "investment" in our kids seems less and less like something that has anything to do with what's best for them.

There is a phrase I often hear—usually incanted like some mystical prayer—that both precedes and proceeds from the spending of innumerable weekends in stuffy gymnasiums and sun-scorched soccer fields: "I mean, they're your kids; you gotta do it, right?" Whenever someone says this to me, I now add "Or else!" to the end of this sentence. I do so for two reasons: (1) I am an insufferable asshole roughly 60 percent of the time, and (2) the phrase "They're your kids; you gotta do it" is an internalization of our religious fidelity to the free market and the altar of scarcity upon which we sacrifice everyone and everything in the hopes of becoming happy or, at the least, less miserable. However, despite the investment, "happiness," in this system at least, remains frustratingly elusive and ill defined. Research and good ole gut-level intuition actually bear this out. A 2016 study published in the *Journal of Family Relations* uncovered an inverse relationship between the amount of monetary investment by parents into youth sports and the level of enjoyment experienced by their children. According to the self-report of the children surveyed, their "lack of enjoyment" was primarily connected to the constant presence of what the authors labeled "pressure." In lay terms, the more cash you spend on your daughter's soccer team, the less likely she's enjoying it.

But let's be honest: you already knew that watching an adult scream "Loser!" at his seven-year-old for striking out isn't terribly helpful for anyone but that kid's future therapist. Just like you needn't be a school superintendent to realize that the 146 percent increase in the time elementary schoolers ages six through eight spent studying over the twenty-year period between 1981 and 2003 probably had very little to do with outcome research into child well-being. Just like you already know that raising kids as investments for which we expect a tidy return in a literal hellscape of outsized expectations, melting ice caps, decreasing opportunities, and increasing competition is the very definition of cruel and unusual. I know this because it happened to me. I'm a millennial, and arguably few other generations have been so thoroughly baptized (and later crucified) by this narrative of relentlessly competitive pressure quite like my own.

EVERYONE HATES MILLENNIALS—
INCLUDING MILLENNIALS

On a person-to-person level, generational stereotypes are notoriously fickle explainers of the human experience. All individuals, through the accident of birth and the odd cocktail of family influences, trauma, and chance encounters, possess a beautiful uniqueness that will always far outpace the unflagging efforts of researchers and marketers. However, as it concerns my own birth cohort and the two generations immediately preceding it, we have seen a rapid weaponization of what it means to be a "boomer" or a "millennial" (or even a forgotten "Gen Xer"). Instead of tepidly serving as some sort of bar graph on a Nielsen presentation, these terms are now often hurled or spat at others in popular discourse, and they have become tidy explanations for malfeasance, racism, entitlement, and the wholesale destruction of American life. If you don't believe me, please consider articles like "American Millennials Are among the World's Least Skilled" or "How the Baby Boomers—Not Millennials—Screwed America." And those represent just the sharpest tip of a much larger internet iceberg I saved you from hitting with your perfectly enjoyable weeknight.

As I mentioned at the outset, a helpful rule of thumb whenever we find ourselves face-to-face with the quaking angst of our reeling populace isn't to demonize or withdraw from one another but to follow the pain because the pain is a mirror back to ourselves, both conscious and unconscious.

Millennials in particular directly express the gnawing ache that accompanies what it is like to be raised as an investment that fails to produce an appropriate return. If you are at all concerned about what awaits our current crop of teenagers with anxiety disorders once they reach adulthood, please consider us millennials your sneak peek. Millennials were a generation almost universally raised to "do anything" and "be everything," with the assumption that we would find ourselves meaningfully fulfilled by existentially weighty and lucrative work. Unlike our parents and grandparents, who faced early generational struggles, millennials were taught to believe that the world was ours and that it was flexible enough to be bent to our will if we would only work hard enough. Technology was supposed to increase our reach and connection, and education was to be the means by which we would continue the upward market trajectory of earning and becoming more than our generational forebears could have imagined at our age. Journalist Anne Helen Petersen sums up millennials thusly: "We were raised to believe that if we worked hard enough, we could win the system—of American capitalism and meritocracy—or at least live comfortably within it. But something happened in the late 2010s. We looked up from our work and realized, there's no winning the system when the system itself is broken."

I heard once from another millennial that growing up as we did was like being raised on a treadmill on which the speed gradually increases, and for a while, we dutifully keep up. But as we age and our knees begin to ache, we notice that the speed keeps going up and up and up. I'm told that lobsters in pots of slowly boiling water have similar realizations but far too late.

Once again, Malcolm Harris poignantly describes the unique context in which my generation has come of age: "Over the past forty years we have witnessed an accelerated and historically unprecedented pace of change as capitalism emerged as the single dominant mode of organizing society. It's a system based on speed, and the speed is always increasing. . . . Lately, this system has started to hyperventilate."

In the midst of larger socioeconomic forces, millennials have begun delaying or altogether eschewing things like child-rearing, marriage, home ownership, steady careers, and much else of what were once believed to be the predictable accouterments of higher education. Mirroring the aforementioned rise of income inequality in our country, millennials are the first generation since the Great Depression to fail to make more money on average than the generation immediately preceding them. These numbers look far worse for millennials of color and for those bereft of Putnam's trinity of social capital, generational wealth, and parents who went to college. As sociologist Tressie McMillan Cottom argues, "In 2020, Black Americans can legally access the major on-ramps to opportunity—college, workplaces, public schools, neighborhoods, transportation, electoral politics—but despite hustling like everyone else, they do not have much to show for it." The market is what raised us, taught us, and, it now seems, is punishing us for our failure to produce a return on all that was invested in us. By most accounts, millennials are failures, and we know it.

Despite what you may have heard about our love of "participation trophies," it's hard to describe the kind of self-flagellation involved in being a millennial in America. Arguably, no one hates millennials more than millennials. It is why we are so very depressed and anxious. And why we report some of the lowest levels of relational well-being in the world (one-fifth of American millennials report that they have no friends). A great many of us represent the most educated and invested-in generation of humans to enter adulthood in the history of our globe. Yet with every economic downturn, our hardscrabble existence is but one more painful reminder of how not-well we are all doing despite being smart, creative, and hardworking. Millennials are the physical evidence that American exceptionalism is and has always been a lie, no matter the amount of money, pressure, and effort one puts into the professionalization of childhood. And the rise of a near-nationwide psychological unwellness accompanying our generation is yet one more example of the ways in which our fundamental not-okayness has been internalized as a deserving punishment for our failures to succeed.

As this bottleneck of opportunity continues to shrink, excluding more and more of an ever-growing stock of the best and brightest from "the good life" in America, our options for creative resistance become equally pinched. "Most of us would rather read a book than stare at our phones," Anne Helen Petersen notes, "but we're so tired that mindless scrolling is all we have energy to do." Whether manifesting as a sort of exhausting, dystopian rage or a cynically resigned withdrawal, our internalized sense of failure is frequently exacerbated by something we were told would save us, connect us, and free us but hasn't: the internet. Maybe if we keep pulling "down to refresh" long enough, though, salvation might one day find us.

3

Why Is Everyone Yelling on the Internet?

How People Became Brands

As the Internet grows . . . like, at a certain point, we're gonna have to build some machinery, inside our guts, to help us deal with this. Because the technology is just gonna get better and better and better and better. And it's gonna get easier and easier, and more and more convenient, and more and more pleasurable, to be alone with images on a screen, given to us by people who do not love us but want our money. Which is all right. In low doses, right? But if that's the main staple of your diet, you're gonna die. In a meaningful way, you're going to die.

—David Foster Wallace, in *Although of Course You End Up Becoming Yourself*

There was a rote and almost liturgical quality to the ways Americans experienced the four bawdy and dystopian years we all spent under the rule of our spray-tanned, half-hearted autocrat and his ALL CAPS Twitter fiats. We would wake up and check the news. Eat breakfast and check the news. Drive to work and check the news. Get to work and check the news. Eat lunch and check the news. Work some more and check the news. Shop for groceries and check the news. Go to the bathroom and check the news. Accidentally drop our phone in the toilet and check the news on the computer. Watch TV and check the news. Parent our children and check the news. Try to sleep and check the news. I even typed this paragraph and checked the news. Twice.

Whenever I find myself reflecting back on the nihilistic quality of the Trump presidency (and its ongoing fallout), I am reminded of the incoherent howls that teenagers sometimes make anytime their parents attempt to take away their smartphones. There is this reflexive, guttural rage in the face of what seems like a profound unfairness, followed by a willingness to sacrifice almost anything and anyone on the altar of what these teenagers believe might free them from the shackles of uncaring parental authority—which is probably why I've always assumed everyone was supposed to yell "Make America Great Again," in the same sweaty, anxious way one might violently demand that a teller at the bank empty his till right into the outstretched bag. Despite the tireless efforts at demonizing, scapegoating, and explaining away his presidency as some sort of democratic malfunction, Donald Trump is our stubbornly incoherent pain made flesh. Even if we reject him, Trump remains—like congealing leftovers in the back of the fridge—as evidence of our own not-okayness in a long red tie and a hasty retweet of a Russian bot pretending to be a white nationalist.

When I use the word "our" in the last sentence to describe the pain all of us have endured as Americans living in a country the *Atlantic* describes almost weekly as "a failed state," I'm not being hyperbolic. I'm being apocalyptic. But don't get lost in the weeds of *Left Behind* Reddit threads and panic rooms, because for the ancients, the word *apocalypse* wasn't so much a shorthand way of describing a multibillion-dollar entertainment industrial complex pandering to our basest fears and desires. Instead, an apocalypse (at least in the original Greek) is a way of "uncovering" or "revealing" what runs the world, what keeps us awake in the middle of the night, and what drives our tireless pull to refresh the Twitter feed no matter the cost to ourselves, our sleep, or our democracy.

"When we bring our wits to bear upon apocalyptic expression we find that it has a way of unmasking the fictions we inhabit by breaking down, among other things, our constructs of public and private, political and religious, natural and spiritual." This is how Belmont professor of religion David Dark terms the mostly unacknowledged apocalyptic impulse coursing through the whole of human life. In this vein, the ravages of the Trump presidency both revealed and burned away the subtext around what "we" mean whenever we say things like "we," "they," and "our" in the first place. Much like our knee-jerk revulsion at the anxious and depressed teenagers we live with, Donald Trump laid bare the pain and angst that long predated his fumbling grasp of the presidency.

"We're just so polarized right now!" is one way you may have described how exactly the last ten years have felt. And you'd be right. You also may have posted this dynamite aphorism on Facebook—which, inarguably, is a medium that has toppled governments and human decency and rewired the brains of generations of living, breathing humans forever. Watching folks struggle to name the sources of our polarization on the very site that so often conjures and collects it feels a bit like hearing that old chestnut about how "Guns don't kill people, people kill people." (Coincidentally, this line of thinking always appears on my own Facebook feed whenever some people use guns to kill other people.) I'm saying that in this analogy Facebook is a gun. And I'm also saying that the naiveté of individual people pretending they can use Facebook responsibly—in the face of contested elections and global pandemics—seems to make about as much sense to me as does the attributing of America's gun death epidemic to a dearth of more responsible individual gun owners. I guess in our world the only thing that can stop a bad guy with a Facebook account is a good guy with one too.

In an address to the Web Summit in Lisbon one year after the 2016 election, Trump campaign tech guru Brad Parscale credited Facebook for willingly placing their employees in campaign offices, helping them raise "a lot of money" in a relatively short amount of time and directly educating the Trump campaign staff on how best to use its platform and engage with a wider audience. "If you're going to spend $100 million on social media, a lot of people show up at your office wanting to help you spend that money on their platforms," Parscale said. I don't want to rush to judgment, but when it concerns our nation's baffling polarization, fear, and surprisingly well-organized not-okayness, perhaps the call is coming from inside the house (and maybe even from your bedside table).

Whether appearing as one more episode of grainy cell phone footage of police brutality heaped on bleeding Black bodies, immigrant children in cages at our country's border, or your friend's recent kitchen renovation (all delivered side-by-side in quick succession), there are few clearer examples of our pain made flesh than the ironically fleshless world of social media. In this world, we are greeted by the algorithmic standardization and cynical organizing of human joy and pain formatted into searchable hashtags passed off as activism and lifestyle brands pretending to be people in order to make unconscionable amounts of money for *other* people.

David Dark refers to those things vibrating in our pockets at funerals and keeping us up late into the night as "electric soul molesters" because—and I'll let him take it from here—phones "have a way of robbing you of our presence and robbing us of yours." So in a world where our phones (and the social media apps keeping us glued to them) possess the power to both topple and inaugurate totalitarian regimes, not to mention rudely interrupt dinner, it's best to learn what we're dealing with when we pull down to refresh.

THE REVOLUTION WILL BE STANDARDIZED

In 2005, roughly 5 percent of Americans used social media. By February 2019 that number had risen to 72 percent, with huge gains in Americans over age fifty. The average length of time a human spends looking at his or her social media feed per day is two hours and twenty-four minutes, which represents a rise of fifty-four minutes since 2012. Here in America, that number hovers around two hours spent daily on social networking sites, with Facebook occupying an average of fifty-eight minutes of almost every American's day.

These numbers don't tell a very compelling story unless we understand them in context. It isn't just the increase in time spent on social media that has had such a wide-reaching impact on humanity; it is the way in which our crippling phone and social media addiction desacralizes the physicality of being alive. In his book *Irresistible*, psychologist Adam Alter references the work of tech wellness guru Kevin Holesh's company Moment, which Holesh developed in response to his own growing tech addiction. This app-based service provides daily check-ins, productivity, and creativity coaching, as well as increasingly serious reminders to turn off one's phone after roughly an hour of use. After digging into the raw numbers of Moment's subscribers, Alter discovered that around 88 percent of the app's users were greatly exceeding the "less than one hour daily" recommendation—like the man beside you at the red light who keeps looking down toward the bottom of his steering wheel even when the light turns green. Users "were spending an average of a quarter of their waking lives on their phones—more time than any other daily activity, except sleeping," according to Alter. "Each month almost one hundred hours was lost to checking email, texting, playing games, surfing the web, reading articles, checking bank balances, and so on. Over the average lifetime, that amounts to a staggering eleven years. . . . This sort of overuse is so prevalent that researchers have coined the term *nomophobia* to describe the fear of being without mobile phone contact (an abbreviation of 'no-mobile-phobia')."

For close to two decades, scientist Jaron Lanier has been bearing witness to the calamitous hold social media and our phones have on our attentions and emotions. Lanier refers to the internet-based standardization of human life as a mostly unconscious effort by regular people on smartphones to "design ourselves to suit digital models of us," and he notes a resulting "leaching of empathy and humanity" in our quest for fuller, richer digital lives. To better understand what Lanier means, consider a 2018 study published in the *Journal of Family Medicine and Primary Care*, which found that between 2011 and 2017, "there have been 259 deaths while clicking selfies in 137 incidents." In response, these researchers have suggested the creation of "no selfie zones" in "places such as water bodies, mountain peaks, and over tall buildings to decrease the incidence of selfie-related deaths"—because, I'm assuming, we can't save ourselves from Instagram.

Thanks to something called the "attention economy," the internet in general (and social media in particular) no longer serves and undergirds the functions and flourishing of human life. Think of all this academic research into the negative impacts of phone and social media usage as a far wordier way of saying "Do it for the Gram" while unsafely repositioning ourselves with a selfie stick in front of a sweeping view of the Grand Canyon we can no longer see because we are now facing our smartphone camera. Anecdotally, I must admit there is a quiet pleasure in witnessing another human taking more than twenty pictures of themselves making a pouty face in front of a fountain hand-carved by artisans some seven hundred years earlier. (I think I once tweeted that exact sentence, which, I suppose, says a bit about that "leaching of empathy" Lanier was referencing.)

While I can't speak for you, I have discovered that it has become increasingly difficult to prevent myself from being a jerk on the internet. I mean that it has become increasingly difficult for me not to see other people—you know, the moving profile pictures walking around outside our smartphones—as the totality of whatever they present online. Whether it's my friend's dad, who used to be "nice, in like a quiet sort of way" before I befriended him on Facebook and uncovered his penchant for peddling deep-state conspiracies or my classmate from grad school who reminds me during every major global catastrophe that "the *real* problem is all the methane production from commercial farming." Friendship in my actual life has become more difficult now that I feel like I've seen everyone in their digital underwear. I have even begun noticing my own unconscious recoil from in-person conversations because the person across from me, if I know them on social media, has had the complexity drained out of them. Here's Lanier again on the difficulties of friendship in the age of Facebook: "A real friendship ought to introduce each person to unexpected weirdness in the other. Each acquaintance is an alien, a well of unexplored difference in the experience of life that cannot be imagined or accessed in any way but through genuine interaction. The idea of friendship in database-filtered social networks is certainly reduced from that."

According to tech theorists like Lanier, one of the most subversive components of living most of our lives online is that our ability to be weird—in contradictory, nonmarketable, and digitally unrecognizable ways—is being stolen from us. Arguably, it is this weirdness that serves as the very bedrock of what makes humans undeniably more important than the technology we have worked tirelessly to create and for which we now willingly sacrifice our privacy and selfhood.

I find it hard to use a word other than *addiction* anytime we give thoughtful consideration to our eager willingness to give up so much of our lives for the supposed benefits of an increasingly polarized, anxious and surveilled online "connection." To be clear, it's getting so bad that we had to pass laws to get people to stop scrolling Instagram and checking email while operating a two-ton vehicle in heavy traffic. Some of you are even doing it right now (please stop).

Historian Yuval Noah Harari grimly spells out what he sees as the long-term effects of this oft-unconscious and always-increasing social media engagement: "Currently, humans risk becoming similar to domesticated animals. We have bred docile cows that produce enormous amounts of milk but are otherwise far inferior to their wild ancestors. They are less agile, less curious, and less resourceful. We are now creating tame humans who produce enormous amounts of data and function as efficient chips in a huge data-processing mechanism, but they hardly maximize their human potential."

When we pause long enough amid the wreckage of our smoldering democracy, strained family dinners, motor vehicle accidents, and constant privacy breaches, a simple question arises: Who actually benefits from this kind of life, from this kind of humanity, and from this kind of connection?

THE MEDIUM IS THE MESSAGE

"It's like I'm expected to have this internal PR department quickly craft 'a statement' every time something like this happens" is how a clergyperson described his life to me whenever calamity rips across his social media network. Whether it's an updated profile picture border we adorn in solidarity with a cause, a post written as a way of shedding light on a recent nonprofit donation, or a retweet we hope will once and for all dismantle the police state, humans on the internet aren't so much talking as they are branding to one another—constantly. Communications theorist Marshall McLuhan famously remarked that "the medium is the message." In other words, the means by which we communicate often shape far more of what we hear and experience than the content itself. If there is anything the humans pretending to be brands and the brands pretending to be humans are saying to one another—about both complex and inane topics—it is that "everything is terrible and you're probably an idiot, but sign up for my newsletter (link in bio)!" The unfortunate truth at the core of our digital interactions is that social media specifically is a transactional medium ruled by the self-same market anxiety we see in teenagers burning themselves out in algebra. It's just that instead of salvation as GPAs and scholarships, *this* network translates the manic "more" of our anxious market economy as "attention . . . or else."

The hold of these platforms over our imaginations is never clearer than when we are railing against their influence over our elections, the selling of our personal data to the highest bidders, or the bastardization of our interior lives *on their very feeds*. Market dominance is typically reflected in a monopoly, and social media clearly has a corner on the standardization and algorithmization of the human soul. Through drop-down menus, gifs, memes, and profile pictures, social media neatly organizes and monetizes how one sleeps, dates, believes, thinks, feels, and furnishes a guest room. This information, then, becomes self-referential, creating a feedback loop where it can be difficult to determine where the profile ends and the self's desires for shiplap begins. "These targeted ads are *so* accurate," we marvel—but are they? Or are we, as Harari claims, just slower, more docile, and easier to catalog because most of our political, social, theological, and occupational life has been boiled down to what we do on a screen? Michigan evangelical megachurch pastor turned Southern California surf guru Rob Bell sums up this tail-eating impulse nicely in his bestselling book *Love Wins*: "We shape our God, and then our God shapes us." These days, it seems, if our online gods are anything, they're *very* angry, and so are we.

THE PLATFORM ALWAYS WINS

In his incredibly popular 2015 book *So You've Been Publicly Shamed*, documentarian and writer Jon Ronson spends three years tracking down individuals across the globe who had one thing in common: a high-profile destruction of their personal lives thanks to a misanthropic joke or off-color commentary on the internet. Throughout his conversations with publicly shamed best-selling authors guilty of plagiarism (like Jonah Lehrer) and regular people (like a woman whose life was eviscerated during a transatlantic flight thanks to an ill-advised tweet about AIDS, Africa, and her relative safety as a white person that she posted just before takeoff), Ronson lays bare the heart of our social media mob mentality. "I suppose that when shamings are delivered like remotely administered drone strikes nobody needs to think about how ferocious our collective power might be," Ronson argues. "The snowflake never needs to feel responsible for the avalanche." In every compassionate and deeply engaging interview, Ronson draws out the ways in which social media activates the very worst components of our deincarnate world: "We can lead good, ethical lives, but some bad phraseology in a Tweet can overwhelm it all—even though we know that's not how we should define our fellow humans. What's true about our fellow humans is that we are clever and stupid."

A friend of mine once remarked in the midst of a social media detox that once he unplugged, it was amazing to come alive to a world "where I don't already know if I immediately hate someone because of my news feed. It's like going back in time." One of the most destructive and politically imperiling aspects of social media standardization is the way in which algorithms incessantly amplify negative and enraging content. "Social media is biased, not to the Left or the Right, but downward," writes Lanier. "The relative ease of using negative emotions for the purposes of addiction and manipulation makes it relatively easier to achieve undignified results. . . . Information warfare units sway elections, hate groups recruit, and nihilists get amazing bang for the buck when they try to bring society down."

How this race to the bottom actually plays out has to do with what Lanier terms "value maximization," in which the algorithm begins sorting and "test using" positive content from, say, massive social movements like the Arab Spring or Black Lives Matter to generate more "interactions" throughout the social media landscape on either side of the political spectrum. In so doing, these revolutionary, connective data become an algorithmic tool for enraging "the other side" and ends up creating a pendulum swing of organized, vitriolic pushback that ultimately becomes "harder to dispel than the positive emotions." This leaves Lanier to gloomily note to Noah Kulwin in an interview for *New York Magazine* that "when you have a Black Lives Matter, the result of that is the empowerment of the worst racists and Neo-Nazis in a way that hasn't been seen in generations. When you have an Arab Spring, the result ultimately is the network empowerment of ISIS and other extremists—bloodthirsty, horrible things, the likes of which haven't been seen in the Arab world or in Islam for years, if ever."

Let's be clear: it isn't that these positive social movements are flawed or somehow inviting of the backlash they receive. In many cases, these online gathering spaces and movements (like Black Lives

Matter, #MeToo, and the Women's March) have effectively mobilized millions of people and resources in an effort to combat systemic and carceral racism, violence against women, and police brutality. They have amplified and connected the voices of countless oppressed populations in their justice-seeking efforts. To overlook the work these online collectives have been able to accomplish through social media is to close ourselves off from the complexity of our world. This is especially true when I remember, as a cisgendered white guy from East Tennessee, how little of my time on earth finds itself assailed by state legislative bodies, white nationalists, and whole subsections of American Christianity willing to elect a predatory reality TV show host to the highest office in the land.

At the same time, I wish simply to note that the medium of social media is also its message, and the message is engagement with the medium at all costs, no matter the kind of content (or world) that results. Either way, whether in boosting the voices of transgendered teens or the Klan, whether in apocalypse or utopia, whether in feast or famine, the platform—or the market, I should say—always wins.

The uniqueness of your humanity, your eccentricity, and your willingness to entertain contradictory or seemingly incompatible ideas about the world simultaneously—all find themselves irrelevant for the great sorting process we undergo every time we pull down to refresh. Much like Jake from North Carolina, whom we met in chapter 2, the anger and anxiety are a kind of fuel—both online and in real life—keeping us plugged into the attention economy out of a fear of failure, missing out, or, worse, irrelevancy. And counterintuitively, the more time we spend in interactions online, the less understanding and understood we become. Without corporeal forms reflecting back to us the pain of our words and actions, there can be no true repentance, no real empathy.

Alter notes a dwindling of empathy in college students over the last thirty years, resulting from, among other things, a diminishing lack of immediate physical feedback in how "our actions affect other people." As our lives continue to be profiled on the internet, we are becoming but empty signals: strangers to ourselves and to one another. The social media algorithms serve to heighten this estrangement by curating an utterly unique news feed that only you can see. In short, walking in my shoes (even if they are Allbirds you also heard about on Spotify) remains an impossibility for a world in which we are constantly connected but to no one in particular.

Arguably, this near-constant feed of loneliness and fearmongering was never the stated goal of the billionaires in hoodies who built our online universe; however, our regular engagement most certainly was. Nothing keeps folks hooked like rage, angst, and a collective loneliness we are occasionally able to keep at bay with unpredictable and episodic online feedback. You might say our global not-okayness is both the price we pay *for* and what we seek to assuage *with* our digital connections. For Facebook and Twitter, bad news is actually good news—or good business, I should say.

In quieter moments between doom scrolls—like when your phone dies at the airport and all the outlets are taken—a thought may have crept into your head: What if I didn't keep doing this? What if I quit using social media as a primary form of human connection? What if I quit checking my email on the weekends and stopped responding to text messages within seconds? What if I ceased giving away my own personal information as well as the personal information of my children on the internet for free as a way of one day securing a following, some reward I can't really articulate, or some sense of belonging and understanding from people I don't even know?

I'm probably not expressing anything that you haven't thought when you are in your right mind. As Arabella discovers in Michaela Coel's award-winning series about sexual violence and the internet, *I May Destroy You*, sometimes even well-intentioned online advocacy ends up laying waste to everything and everyone around us. All of us know we need to quit or cut down on our use of social media. Our democracy demands it. Our families demand it. Our mental health demands it. *But we can't*, especially now that most of our shopping, our spiritual formation, the ongoing maintenance of our relationships, as well as much of our current and future work are increasingly digitized. As Simon Peter reminds Jesus in the Gospel of John, "To whom would we go? You have the words of eternal life" (John 6:68 NET).

Even in writing this book, I am forced to tweet and post on Facebook about it, to curate a half-hearted connection to people I don't know on the internet in hopes that they'll buy my work, maintain a connection to it, and tweet and post on Facebook about it within their own spheres of social media influence. *I can't leave, even if I want to, because Zuckerberg has the words of eternal life and every restaurant lists their current hours on Facebook.* The good news—that anyone can be successful, famous, or a global or local change agent or go viral on the internet—is actually terrible news because it necessitates a connection to something that drains the complexity of life and sacrifices it on the altar of our digital salvation. We think all this is going to somehow save us, even if it kills in the process.

Having grown up as an evangelical Christian in East Tennessee, I am intimately familiar with this kind of sacrificial faith—except that I was taught to call this lack of okayness we've spent the last two chapters outlining a "God-shaped hole" in my soul. This is a folksy way of describing what Augustine once called a constant state of "restlessness" that can only find rest and fulfillment in God. My tradition believed that all of us were born with a fundamental lack of okayness, or restlessness. We were taught to call this restlessness "original sin," and we believed it could only be satisfied by a "personal relationship" with the one true God. Outside of God, we would continue to live a life of painful longing, dissatisfaction, loneliness, and eventual torment for all of eternity in a place called hell.

To avoid this grisly fate, regular engagement with and reflection on my ongoing sinfulness, lostness, and brokenness was the only way to maintain a proper amount of gratitude toward this God. This, in reality, should be rightly understood as a self-interested effort in thinking terrible, toxic, and anxious thoughts about myself in order to eventually secure this God's blessing, favor, and salvation.

Sound familiar? Regular, painful engagement with the bad news of our bottomless depravity—you could call it existential doom scrolling—is the "good news"; it is what will eventually save us, even if it kills us in the process. I later came to find out my spiritual tradition most certainly pinpointed the right universally anxious emptiness but, perhaps, the wrong God at the center of it.

4

Why Does Heaven Seem So Out of Reach?

How Capitalism Became Religion

The capitalist-consumerist ethic is revolutionary. . . . The new ethic promises paradise on condition that the rich remain greedy and spend their time making more money, and that the masses give free rein to their craving and passions—and buy more and more. This is the first religion in history whose followers actually do what they are asked to do. How, though, do we know that we'll really get paradise in return? We've seen it on television.

—Yuval Noah Harari, *Sapiens*

When I was three years old, my parents split up. Don't feel too bad for me; only 45.8 percent of American children make it to age seventeen while still living with both of their parents. At least my mom and biological father had the foresight to take me to Disney World before dismantling our little family (where, I am told, I had a wonderful time). This sudden interruption of life as I had known it brought a multitude of accompanying challenges and changes—one of which went by "David" and strangely only showed up at my mom's house to play with me and my Lego pirate ship right before the babysitter arrived.

Language is a funny thing. Sometimes you don't really have a way of articulating the profundity of what you're going through until you hear someone else say it out loud. In these moments it's as if the whole of your formerly inarticulate experience comes rushing at you all at once. Words like *cancer* or *divorce* have a way of laying bare the cold realities of what you have actually been experiencing, even if you were unable to admit it to yourself. For me, *stepfather* was one of these words. Much like the Trump presidency and the heaving not-okayness of anxious American teenagers, the word *stepfather* apocalyptically burned away the fictions I had been quietly harboring about getting the family band back together. Donning a cummerbund and white carnation to join the bridal party of my mother's second marriage to a second David (yes, my biological father's name was *also* David) mostly finished the job.

Over the course of our new relationship, my stepfather would introduce me to many things about being a human that I had been unfamiliar with before his arrival. One of those things was how to hit a curveball and another was exactly how many unread newspapers could fit in the back of a 1989 Honda Civic without causing the bumper to scrape on speed bumps. Most importantly, he taught me how to patiently and quietly love a son who, for the first twenty-five or so years, understood him as little more than the frustrating replacement for a biological father who was never really there. I'm saying that I gave David a lot of shit, and he gave a bit back, but we had an agreement and mostly it was fine. But then my stepfather met my newborn son and fell asleep with him in his arms and is now teaching him to hit a baseball in the backyard while I watch. And I am nothing if not forever grateful for the way he kindly ruined my life.

One unconquerable value I quickly discovered my new dad held was the role that "sales" could and should play in a free market society. How this played out directly was in his seemingly cellular grasp of the differences separating a "good deal" from a "bad deal." While my mother and I typically remained confused anytime he came home from "running to the store" for something we didn't ask for, the mathematics behind David's deal-making seemed airtight. A good deal was getting one hundred things for one hundred dollars, and a bad deal was getting only one thing for one hundred dollars (unless that one thing was a power tool). Often this was a great way to buy groceries (well, sort of) but less helpful when it came time to shop for new school clothes or make other much larger non-power-tool purchases.

A second, equally important value during my tutelage in consumption under David's watchful eye can be summed up by the golden rule of capitalism: "the customer is always right." Originally coined in the early 1900s by English entrepreneur Harry G. Selfridge, "the customer is always right" served as a way of engendering both customer loyalty and employee fidelity to his London department store. In the hands of the English, one imagines a *Downton Abbey*-esque quality to customer service interactions at Selfridge's around the turn of the twentieth century. However, when employed by red-blooded Americans—my stepfather occasionally included—this mantra of the free market allows one the liberty of yelling loudly at retail workers, refusing to tip service staff, requesting to see managers, bringing expired coupons to the store, or stridently returning purchases as a hard-earned expression of one's inalienable consumer rightness.

This kind of quietly internalized capitalism raised me, and it raised you. It is the air we breathe, the God we pray to, the blessing we seek, and the water in which we constantly swim. It's time we started naming it.

WHAT THE HELL IS WATER?

In a now famous speech to the 2005 graduating class of Kenyon College, America's wordiest genius, David Foster Wallace, describes the experience of two young fish swimming together only to be passed by a much older fish, who kindly remarks, "Mornin', boys, how's the water?" This unexpected greeting leaves one of the young fish to turn to the other with a question for the ages: "What the hell is water?"

Wallace goes on to elucidate that an old-fashioned liberal arts education is rooted in the practice of cultivating awareness, or an attention to the facts, philosophies, and theologies under which one orders life, makes grocery lists, and fumes in heavy traffic at the end of the workday. As his graduation remarks reach their close, Wallace turns wistfully sermonic:

> In the day-to-day trenches of adult life, there is actually no such thing as atheism. There is no such thing as not worshipping. Everybody worships. The only choice we get is *what* to worship. And an outstanding reason for choosing some sort of God or spiritual-type thing to worship—be it J. C. or Allah, be it Yahweh or the Wiccan mother-goddess or the Four Noble Truths or some infrangible set of ethical principles—is that pretty much anything else you worship will eat you alive. If you worship money and things—if they are where you tap real meaning in life—then you will never have enough. Never feel you have enough. It's the truth. Worship your own body and beauty and sexual allure and you will always feel ugly, and when time and age start showing, you will die a million deaths before they finally plant you. . . . The insidious thing about these forms of worship is not that they're evil or sinful; it is that they are unconscious. They are default-settings. . . . We have to keep reminding ourselves, over and over: "This is water. This is water."

Talking frankly in America about the rites, rigors, and rituals of capitalism—or even what the hell capitalism is—feels unsettling at first, much like what hearing the word *stepfather* did to me the first time someone said it about the new David I had been playing with a few times each week. This strange sensation—confusion, really—at having your unconscious capitalist infant baptism finally confirmed is what naturally results whenever we young fish hear about water for the first time.

In my therapy practice, I am often reminded of the pain that can accompany both the naming and the questioning of something a patient has previously believed to be as unimpeachable as gravity and air. When you leave a religious tradition—even one disguised as pure economic theory—it is normal to experience a lightheadedness, anger, and deep longing as you encounter formerly unconsidered alternative possibilities and lost time. My use of the term "religious tradition" here is purposeful because religion is exactly what we're really talking about whenever we talk about our collective pain under capitalism. Shame, anxiety, and an internalized responsibility for everything from your parents' divorce to the market contraction of your industry is, frankly, a rather religiously held sentiment. This is doubly true whenever you invite adherents to begin doubting these unquestioned beliefs.

In his landmark book *The Powers That Be*, theologian Walter Wink pinpoints the role our fidelity to individualism plays in furthering the unconscious internalization of our market-mandated pain: "One legacy of the rampant individualism in our society is the tendency to react personally to the pain caused by institutions. People blame themselves when they get downsized. Or they blame the executive officers for their insensitivity. But to a high degree, corporate decisions are dictated by larger economic forces—invisible forces that determine the choices of those who set policy and fire workers."

I've found, as both pastor and psychotherapist, that it's terribly difficult to offer a therapeutic response to something that is equal parts inescapable and unnameable. But as Wallace pastorally begs, "We have to keep reminding ourselves, over and over: This is water. This is water."

IT'S NOTHING PERSONAL; IT'S JUST BUSINESS

In his breathless treatise *Capitalist Realism: Is There No Alternative?*, the late English philosopher Mark Fisher lays bare what he calls a gradual "naturalization" of capitalism from "value" to "fact." Fisher argues that principles and ideologies can "never be really successful" until they effectively transition from values people choose to hold to facts they are unable to question or escape. "Over the past thirty years, capitalist realism has successfully installed a 'business ontology' in which it is simply obvious that everything in society, including healthcare and education, should be run as a business," he writes. For those of us who didn't graduate from Kenyon College with a double major in anthropology and indie rock, *ontology* is a way of describing the study of how people understand themselves as beings in the world. It's an academic way of describing what we talk about whenever we find ourselves lying with close friends on the hood of a Thunderbird staring up at the night sky.

Fisher uses the word *ontology* to describe what it's like to have our insatiable capitalist system internalized to the point that it begins to colonize our entire sense of being. When capitalism is internalized, it becomes nearly impossible to understand who and what we are independent of its actuarial logic—for example, "it's nothing personal; it's just business." On the face of it, this makes total sense, except that in a world where everything is business, the personal—the truly intimate components of our families, our health, our privacy, our safety, and even our selfhood—is almost certainly for sale. Hell, here in America, even our racism is capitalist. In his best-selling call to action *How to Be an Antiracist*, Ibram X. Kendi rightly identifies capitalism as the "conjoined twin" of racism. Capitalism provides the foundational environmental factors necessary for racism to freely germinate: "To love capitalism is to end up loving racism. To love racism is to end up loving capitalism. The conjoined twins are two sides of the same destructive body. The idea that capitalism is merely free markets, competition, free trade, supplying and demanding, and private ownership of the means of production operating for a profit is as whimsical and ahistorical as the White-supremacist idea that calling something racist is the primary form of racism."

From the professionalization of childhood to the co-opting of social movements and human relationships on social media to the wholesale degradation and privatization of institutional support systems like schools and health care, the market makes it difficult to discern where exactly business ends and the personal begins. For instance, during the early days of the global pandemic of 2020, a popular rallying cry of conservatives in America was that we should reopen our shuttered economy and bravely return "to normal" out of a dogged fidelity to the health of the market. The assertion of normalcy by these free market devotees ranged from refusing to wear masks or practice social distancing, on the one hand, to openly protesting health restrictions and lockdowns with assault rifles in front of city hall, on the other.

This logic was employed in direct contradiction to existing data on the rapid community spread of the coronavirus—not to mention its continued ravaging of our most aged and health-compromised citizens—out of a commitment to something "more important than living," as then lieutenant governor of Texas Dan Patrick cynically put it just two months into the spread of the novel coronavirus here in the United States: "We are crushing the economy. . . . There are more important things than living. And that's saving this country for my children and my grandchildren and saving this country for all of us." In the face of possible economic collapse, Americans—from nursing home residents to delivery drivers—were invited to become religiously sacrificial. To be clearer, we were being asked to willingly strap life, limb, and vulnerable loved ones to the altar of our economy in order to save something "more important than living."

Throughout the early days of the pandemic, I found myself inundated with hagiographic accounts of tireless health care workers and "essential" fast-food employees serving our country during "wartime" (as our then president sort of put it). The sentimental footage of humans selflessly and creatively serving one another under frightful circumstances provided a helpful respite—or at least "some good news" during our country's bipolar efforts at curtailing the spread of the virus. As the pandemic wore on, however, the frequency of good news faded—or, more specifically, was sold to CBS/Viacom. In its absence, we were left with the harsh realization that the market we were attempting to bravely prop up had left all of us dangerously exposed to a virus other countries were effectively curtailing with rapid, widespread, and effectively administered public health initiatives. We were truly on our own.

Yes, the *Mad Max* feel of wiping down milk cartons with bleach wipes, alone on my front porch in a surgical mask after grocery shopping, did make me feel less connected to my neighbors and other citizens. But even that was nothing compared to what I felt when hearing from the elected officials charged with overseeing our public safety that the only thing capable of saving "our way of life" is the sacrificial death of myself or my loved ones in service to the market.

I misspoke earlier. There is nothing personal anymore because it's all business—or maybe it's all *religion*.

YOU SHOULD BE DEPRESSED

After loaning money to her parents to help cover the utility bill, a teenager I'll call Jane once asked me, "Is it still depression, Eric, when you get so tired of thinking about how your dad makes less an hour than you do at your fast-food job that you just want to scream and cry all day?"

Yes is the answer to this student's question about the psychologically depressing effects of living in the midst of economically insecure circumstances—and no too. We probably should avoid clinically pathologizing the accompanying pain of poverty as the result of some sort of individual failure of will or biology because the truth is more complicated than that. In his book *This City Is Killing Me*, Chicago-based social worker Jonathan Foiles perfectly encapsulates the inherent tension of diagnosing mental illness in a profoundly unequal society: "We diagnose people, not cultures or neighborhoods, with depression. This singular focus can help obscure the environmental factors that contribute to mental illness and minimize the contributions our society makes to the mental suffering of the poor. It is far easier to feel depressed if you live in a neighborhood that has experienced chronic disinvestment, has few supportive community resources available, and is marred by gun violence."

The pain this student and many others across the socioeconomic spectrum are bearing witness to has far less to do with serotonin deficits and the proper application of cognitive behavioral therapy and far more to do with what Fisher terms the "privatization of stress." This, he argues, is a market-driven dismantling of our health care industry's collective responsibility to provide ethical and effective care in favor of a system ruled by competition and the accumulation of capital at all costs. In taking this line of thinking to its logical conclusions, Fisher demands a "reframing" or "politicization" of mental health disorders. In this frame, depression and anxiety are viewed less as commonplace disorders capriciously impacting the lives of individuals and more as hard evidence of capitalism's inherent dysfunction. He notes, "The 'mental health plague' in capitalist societies would suggest that, instead of being the only social system that works, capitalism is inherently dysfunctional, and that the cost of it appearing to work is very high."

In *Caring for Souls in a Neoliberal Age*, Bruce Rogers-Vaughn cites the work of researchers Richard Wilkinson and Kate Pickett, who analyzed global income inequality and social well-being by comparing data from the twenty-three richest economies in the world. Wilkinson and Pickett note that low measures of social well-being—such as high rates of mental illness and obesity, as well as an accompanying decline in childhood educational performance and social mobility, among others—correlate with a country's steepening income inequality. Despite having the strongest gross domestic product (GDP) in the world, the United States scored the lowest in terms of social well-being out of the twenty-three countries in Wilkinson and Pickett's study, with especially grim numbers of citizens suffering from pervasive mental illness and addiction. These findings lead Rogers-Vaughn to note, glibly, that "the neoliberalization [read: 'free marketization'] of a society leads to increased levels of inequality, which in turn signals an increase in human suffering of all types."

If anything, living in this kind of world *should* be anxiety-inducing and depressing because, much like our addiction to our phones, the pain is kind of the point. It's what keeps us engaged with the platform (in this case, capitalism): internalizing the stress, working weekends, and constantly avoiding failure. Despite being regularly invited to talk to your primary care physician about a new antidepressant you heard about on TV, the depression and anxiety aren't actually the problem. They are, instead, a way of baldly drawing our attention to the destructive reality in which we're all living.

In a 2019 paper, biological anthropologists Kristen Syme and Edward Hagen argue that the "chemical imbalance" model successfully disseminated by the pharmaceutical industry "via direct-to-consumer advertising" curtailed a fuller understanding of how depression and anxiety could be more holistically understood in the lives of sufferers. As a corrective, Syme and Hagen refer to anxiety and depression as "adverse but possibly adaptive defenses" that help sufferers to "avoid future such adversities." Put more simply, think of anxiety as the initial energy rush accompanying a traumatic experience and depression as the resultant retraction or immobilization of this hopefulness in the face of situations outside of our control.

This recharacterization of our anxious or depressive pain as initially useful leads Syme and Hagen to argue that disorders of "low heritability, caused by adversity, and involv[ing] symptoms that seem to be adaptive responses to adversity"—like depression and anxiety—should be treated with "social, not medical, solutions" because they clearly indicate "social problems."

In realizing what swimming in this kind of water has done to us, our commitment to internalized productivity and competition at all costs—like any fundamentalist tradition—hasn't always been orthodox. It was once just a theory among many for how capitalism and democracy should coexist. People called it neoliberalism.

COMPETITION IS NEXT TO GODLINESS

You just read the word *neoliberalism*. Perhaps you—like me, coming across any art museum's description of a particular artist's "motivations"—found yourself thinking, "I know what these words mean, discretely, but not when you combine them like that." So let me (try to) speak plainly: neoliberalism is the concerted socio-political effort to shift capitalism from a tightly regulated system of market exchange into a freewheeling, deregulated, and totalizing force erasing any and every boundary between nations, societies, and selves in order to unshackle the market. This form of capitalism inhabits you, controls the movements of your industry, invites you to post pictures of your son's birthday party on Instagram, and sends countries into war. It is as ubiquitous as water.

Historian Eugene McCarraher characterizes neoliberalism as the establishment of "one vast and ecumenical holding company" and tracks its rise from a small protest movement of academics and business leaders forged in response to New Deal economic policies in the 1940s to its eventual dismantling of the welfare state and organized labor under the watchful eyes of Reagan and Thatcher in the 1980s and Blair and Clinton in the 1990s. McCarraher argues that capitalism became something more than mere economic policy and represents what he calls an "attempt to remake all of human life in the crucible of capital accumulation, right down to the recesses of personal identity." This occurred not only in the halls of power with the disempowerment of financial regulatory bodies but also in the very hearts and souls of American citizens. Politicians began utilizing the language of magic, theology, and utopia to describe the wisdom of the market in setting our civilization's course. As Ronald Reagan put it in 1982, "There really is something magic about the marketplace when it's free to operate."

McCarraher characterizes this neoliberal shift as further evidence of a thoroughgoing "enchantment" of money itself, which fills the spiritual vacuum left behind by our crumbling institutional religious bodies: "Under capitalism, money occupies the ontological *[there's that word again]* throne from which God has been evicted." No matter our explicit rejection of any religion's hold over us as a nation, we are a sacramental people, and as Wallace reminded us earlier, "there is no such thing as not worshipping."

How else than as religious devotion might we understand our willingness to unquestioningly persist in the cold calculations of a winner-take-all economic system? Almost 67 percent of American bankruptcies in 2018 were due to health care costs incurred from a medical system that paid its sixty-two wealthiest CEOs a combined 1.1 billion dollars in compensation that same year. How is this anything but evidence of the enshrinement of accumulation and competition as moral imperatives? Whether depicted in our disavowal of comfort in the face of success (exemplified profoundly in the Super Bowl–winning quarterback "getting right back to work" after winning the big game) or in our constant internalization of failure, the one economic constant is our pain.

Alternating states of depression and anxiety are what it feels like when humans live as businesses, brands, or investments that must manage themselves online and turn a profit each quarter. For many of my teenage patients, it isn't so much a question of eliminating these feelings as of surviving them and therefore avoiding a further diminishment of their work output, grades, and future earning potential. Even the very words *depression* and *anxiety* have been so thoroughly infused with market-derived meaning that their mere appearance in clinical documentation often determines the pace, frequency, and interventions available to a treating therapist—depending, of course, on a patient's deductible.

In the words of the polite insurance auditor reviewing my treatment of a "depressed" adolescent attempting to survive catastrophic loss and family chaos amid a global pandemic, "Normally, effective treatment would see a reduction in appointments over the last ten months, but you're still seeing this patient weekly. Please tell us why." Surgery options, available hospitals, treating physicians, and even the fifty minutes you spend behind a closed door with your therapist each week: these are all left to the wisdom of our Market God.

THE PAIN IS MANDATORY

Across the socioeconomic landscape, the fundamental lack of okay-ness so many of us toil under isn't just an unfortunate side effect of our tireless grasping at success; it is a necessary condition for the maintenance of the market itself. Despite your preferred religious tradition's best efforts at characterizing your resting discontent as morally depraved greed, the bottomless ache interrupting family vacations and the birthday parties of our children with the news that someone on Instagram did it better, and with more succulents, is equal parts byproduct and lifeblood of the market.

Discontentment is both capitalism's oxygen and its carbon dioxide. The pain demands we respond to it by competing for increasingly scarce resources in order to consume products we don't need as a way of providing a momentary respite before the market-mandated discontent arises once again, usually thanks to a cursory scroll through social media when the workday ends.

From the apps giving us up-to-the-minute updates on our credit scores to teenagers dry heaving their way through calculus, and from the repeated shuttering of failing schools in underfunded neighborhoods to the constant refreshing of our email during a restless night and the habitual greeting "So, what do you do for a living?"—the invisible hand of the market is always heavy upon us. In the moments between work and Target and checking email on my phone in the background of almost every life experience, my doubt starts creeping in once again, and I begin wondering quietly to myself, "So the customer is *always* right? The market is *always* right?"

"It's easier to imagine the end of the world" is how political philosophers Slavoj Žižek and Fredric Jameson described the experience of entertaining the end of capitalism. Nearly forty years earlier, Margaret Thatcher famously characterized the environmentally inescapable role capitalism plays in the maintenance of Western democracies with her famous aphorism "Capitalism: there is no alternative." Thatcher intoned this slogan so frequently that the British media eventually referred to her by the acronym TINA as a way of brusquely referring to her fervent free market orthodoxy.

I use this word *orthodoxy* on purpose—namely, because I struggle to find a different way of articulating the kind of religious devotion required of parents who willingly participate in the professionalization of childhood. Or the kind of religious devotion it takes to blindly click "I agree" to literally any collection of paragraphs elucidating the electronic buying and selling of our privacy and selfhood. Or the kind of religious devotion it takes to "happily" live in a country where Black citizens are accosted, jailed, or killed with impunity by police or immigrant children are separated from their parents and kept in cages at our southern border out of a desire for "security," "protection," and an ever-tenuous grasp on "prosperity."

Drawing clear correlations between the toxic stress in modern America and a worldview valorizing near-feudal levels of wealth inequality is difficult both because of the collective unconsciousness of our free market orthodoxy and, perhaps more insidiously, because of the violent rejection of any admittance of our doubt. For instance, in American political life, a politician's open criticism of capitalism not only eliminates his or her viability for high public office—as democratic socialist Bernie Sanders discovers every four years or so—but also awakens rage at anything disparaging our country's religious fidelity to the market. Sermonizing for his parishioners on Fox News, high priest Sean Hannity apocalyptically outlines the fate awaiting all of us were capitalism to be thoroughly dismantled by politicians like Bernie Sanders or New York congresswoman Alexandria Ocasio-Cortez: "They want to decide what you eat, what you say, where you live and how you make your living and how much you can make. . . . Sounds familiar? It should because this kind of all-powerful, centralized, socialist, statist government has been tried all over the world and it has resulted—every single solitary time, without exception—in nothing but suffering and carnage for the people they promised to help so much."

When conceived of as an unimpeachable force for good in the struggle for the soul of a democratic nation-state and its citizens, capitalism isn't really an economic system at all anymore; it's something far more elemental, even sacred.

JUST ONE MORE QUARTER

In his book *The Market as God*, Harvey Cox deftly defines our country's worshipful posture toward the market: "Faith in the workings of the markets actually takes the form of a functioning religion, complete with its own priests and rituals, its own doctrines and theologies, its own saints and prophets, and its own zeal to bring its gospel to the whole world and win converts everywhere. The fact that acolytes of the market faith do not formally acknowledge it as a religion does not change this reality." Cox goes on to highlight how the oft-mysterious movements of the market are enfleshed in the competing images of either bear-god or bull-god. "Futures" are tracked by day traders appearing less like well-compensated graduates of Ivy League institutions and more like seers incanting prayers we can't understand. It is the inherent complexity of our economic system and its accompanying indecipherable sacred texts that so often lead us laypeople to seek the advice of those chosen few among us, singled out as worthy of divining the capricious whims of our Market God. *It's all just too big.*

The complexity is why we're often told that no matter where the Dow closes, Wall Street demands the steady delivery of our tithes and offerings. This impulse may explain the motivations behind our government rewarding "the Street" after the 2008 financial crash with a $700 billion government bailout, $1.6 billion of which went to executive bonuses. Whether in growth or recession, the demands of our market and its priests remain stubbornly familiar: *more . . . or else.* Our salvation at the hands of the market always requires sacrificial trust.

In this unquestioned religious system, things like affordability, market share, debt load, and net worth function as a new sort of morality—a divinely ordained credit score that we begin fashioning from birth. The building of a personal resume or brand is part of this effort, as is the constant accrual of social capital, education, possessions, and occupational achievement. We do all of this out of a devotional hope that one day we might finally accomplish enough and earn enough to retire from the struggle and pain of existing in a system where competition and existential restlessness are mandatory.

According to financial management commercials featuring boomers captaining schooners in the middle of the workday, retirement is a kind of heaven. Research is now showing, however, that upon reaching this longed-for Elysium, retirees suddenly become just as susceptible (if not even more so) to mental illness, depression, anxiety, and suicidal ideation as our teenagers.

"We just need more patience," Harari writes, sarcastically aping the answer of capitalism to its many critics. "Paradise, the capitalists promise, is right around the corner. True, mistakes have been made, such as the Atlantic slave trade and the exploitation of the European working class. But we have learned our lesson, and if we just wait a little longer and allow the pie to grow a little bigger, everybody will receive a fatter slice." Our salvation at the hands of the market always requires a sacrificial patience.

Bottomless patience seems the only requirement for surviving the uniquely American inhumanity of attempting to transfer your internet service upon moving or surviving an experience at your local emergency room after cutting your hand open on a can of refried beans. During such times, a quietly apocalyptic awareness emerges of the double-sided truth holding our economic religious tradition together: *you are profoundly alone, and you are definitely getting screwed.*

Today no problem has an answer, no politician an effective policy, and no boss the authority to enact change, because the system is too complicated to manage. This complexity has been meticulously maintained by our country's thorough commitment to the individualization and privatization of responsibility and the dismantling of community structures and collectives that might challenge the deregulated power of our Market God. Once again, Thatcher was prescient in her understanding of capitalism's role in our future, as she famously remarked to the British media in the late 1970s that "there is no society; there are only individuals and families." When put another way, this amounts to *you and your family are on your own, so get back to work until you can't anymore.*

THE CULT OF MINIMAL VARIATION

While the market may position itself as an unimpeachable deity, it is ultimately only an absence, a bottomless lack that creates nothing but guilt. In my work as a therapist, this guilt usually manifests as an insatiable ache for fulfillment that never quite finds what it's looking for no matter how many hours we work, how much we earn, or how many AP classes our kids take. The market is a god whose genesis is found in our collective commitment to the passing on of a generational disappointment—in our lives, our work, and our purchases, as well as ourselves and our children—out of the belief that one day, someone will receive a return on our investment of pain. As the story goes, the pain may be uncomfortable, but it is a decidedly necessary kind of evil because it will eventually save us if only we would use it correctly. In service to this myth, the market keeps us in pain. But as the pain continues increasing, it prevents us from, as Fisher notes, "bold thinking or entrepreneurial leaps" and instead locks us into standardization, "conformity," and what he calls the "cult of minimal variation."

It's hard to have enough juice left in the tank for the future—for alternative ways of being, doing, and believing—when we've got to survive the mountainous paperwork and bottomless choices of the present. Not only is our creativity truncated by our insatiable Market God, but far nobler aims of truth, grace, and peace are greatly reduced by a masochistic expenditure of pain as both the means and the end of market maintenance. For now, there is no longer saved or damned, heaven or hell; there is only *more* or nothing.

As with any unconscious truth—like a shadowy movie villain haunting us from just off-screen—dragging the thing into the light is only the beginning. Holding it responsible: now that's where the real movie magic is.

Like I mentioned earlier, I used to be a pastor. I became one because I was introduced at an early age to the collective power of people caring for one another in the absence of reward. We called this "bearing one another's burdens" in my Southern Baptist tradition. Because of the abundant generosity, love, and faithfulness I experienced in my childhood church, I hung around Christianity long enough to find out that the white guy with long hair in all those Velvet Elvis–esque prints hanging throughout the church building were actually of a brown-skinned Jewish man who didn't speak a lick of English. I even ended up discovering that he was so thoroughly committed to the nonviolent dismantling of oppressive and abusive religious structures that he not only died in order to bring about a new kind of kingdom; he inspired a global movement of outcasts and "sinners" to begin remaking their world in his selfless, sacrificial image. Who knew, right?

Back then, I remember thinking Christianity seemed like a movement capable of building a world worth living in—or, at the least, one worth getting out of bed for before noon on the weekends. Then people started paying me to practice Christianity out loud, for their churches and for their children. It was here that I was brought face-to-face with the true purpose my religious tradition has come to serve in our present world: that of spiritual anesthetic for and existential distraction from the occasional fits of doubt that arise in the continued market maintenance of our pain.

Much like the hollow promises of upward mobility and "real" connection on the internet, dominant white American Christianity, in its present form, is yet one more overprescribed antidepressant. Its endlessly touted relief only comes to us in heaven, a place where the market no longer requires our devotions.

5

Why Does God Seem So Depressed?

How Christianity Became Anesthetic

> To define religion primarily as a quest for personal satis-
> faction or salvation is to make it a refined kind of magic.
> As long as man sees in religion the satisfaction of his
> own needs, a guarantee for immortality or a device to
> protect society, it is not God whom he or she serves,
> but himself. . . . It is a sure way of missing Him when we
> think that God is an answer to a human need, as if not
> only armies, factories, and movies, but God, too, had to
> cater to the ego.
>
> —Abraham Joshua Heschel, *Man Is Not Alone*

The summer after my first year of college, I spent a week in Mexico on a "mission trip" as a member of something called a "youth choir." I realize you may not know what the words "youth choir" or "mission trip" might mean, so I've included several preemptive responses to your inevitable questions.

Yes, our shirts always matched.

No, most of us were quite terrible at Spanish. Our Southern accents only made it worse once we turned the boom box on and started singing along with the prerecorded hymns.

Yes, a "youth choir" is as cool as it sounds.

Yes, roughly 97 percent of us contracted travelers' diarrhea, and we later spoke of our harrowing experience abroad with the very same bravado as your college friend who studied in England for a semester and interrupted every trip to the grocery store thereafter to let you know that "overseas they don't have nearly as many cereal options as you Americans do."

And finally, yes, forty middle-class white kids in matching red T-shirts and Abercrombie khakis singing hymns in Spanish for Mexican audiences who had to strain to decipher the unintelligible words of their own language was incredibly confusing for everyone involved.

As a group of white Americans abroad, our conversations typically orbited around a rather predictable constellation of travelogue topics like food, language, weather, and toilet paper disposal options. However, one consistent point of confusion was the divergence we witnessed between the religious practices of the Mexican Christians with whom we were ministering and those of us middle-class, white Southern Baptists. For with every encounter we had with local liturgies, festivals, holy days, and ceremonies for the dead came a regular refrain from the back row of the air-conditioned minibus: "So, uhhh, these people are Christians too?" This cross-cultural and theological uneasiness was quickly dispatched by a simple phrase used endlessly by Americans on mission trips to foreign lands: "folk religion."

In our case, labeling the spirituality we encountered as "folk religion" was a way to eliminate or bypass the cognitive dissonance that arises anytime white middle-class American Christians discover that "Christianity" means very different things for people who didn't grow up in subdivisions named after trees that were cut down to build our cul-de-sacs. "Folk religion" is a tidy way of putting the more challenging practices, rituals, and behaviors of nonwhite, non-American Christians in their appropriate context. This definition provided a way of understanding how "aberrant expressions," "heresies," or "indigenous beliefs" worked their way insidiously into what we were taught to believe was a more "orthodox" practice of Christianity. Calling something "folk religion" is the *They don't know any better*—or, because I'm from the South, the *Bless your heart*—of interreligious dialogue.

During our conversations as a mission team, there was little mention of the brutal conquering forces responsible for introducing the ancestral peoples of Central and South America to Christianity, let alone how difficult it must have been to receive theological instruction from red-T-shirted teens who eerily resembled said conquering forces. All of that proved moot in the face of more pressing concerns—namely, that for true communion with God to take place, this folk religion must be excised once and for all by a *proper* delivery of what we grew up calling "the gospel" or "the good news."

THE POWER OF ORTHODOXY
AND THE ORTHODOXY OF POWER

Today, with Mexican youth choir stardom squarely in the rearview, I live in East Tennessee. If there's one thing I've found to be true about the religious self-understanding of my ancestral Appalachian home, it's that for a "persecuted" sect of weary Christian pilgrims, there sure are a helluva lot of us down here. In light of Christianity's relative ubiquity, it is to this day more scandalous in East Tennessee to admit a lack of belief in God than it is to fly two oversized Confederate flags on the back of your truck. Yes, I'm saying it's more socially acceptable for an east Tennessean to be a racist than an atheist. Or, to put an even finer point on it, *all* of us white American Christians practice "folk religion," even when we don't consult shamans or believe in the lost cause of the Confederacy.

Ibram X. Kendi deftly defines the ways that the "conjoined twins" of racism and capitalism work to racialize and disenfranchise not only individuals but entire spaces, institutions, and countries: "Just as racist power racializes people, racist power racializes space. The ghetto. The inner city. The third world. A space is racialized when a racial group is known to either govern the space or make up the clear majority in the space. . . . Policies of space racism overresource White spaces and underresource non-White spaces. Ideas of space racism justify resource inequity through creating a radical hierarchy of space, lifting up White spaces as heaven, down-grading non-White spaces as hell." The "hierarchy of space" Kendi outlines not only racializes white and nonwhite spaces—thus further divesting minority communities of resources and opportunity—but also sacralizes this disparity by holding up white spaces and white traditions as exemplars of places and people that are (obviously) blessed by the divine. Or, in the words of first-time dream-home owners in Waco, Texas, with jaws agape at custom kitchen cabinets on HGTV's *Fixer Upper*: "This must be what heaven looks like." For white people surrounded by gleaming shiplap, even the great beyond has quartz countertops and gentrification.

Across white Christian theological and denominational traditions in America, most of our "right beliefs" have very little to do with effective biblical interpretive practices and very much more to do with how capitalism defines the totality of our world and our relationships within it. Anytime middle- and upper-middle-class white American Christians find themselves in underresourced and oppressed communities, an inherent, unquestioned hierarchy privileging our theology, our authority, and our perspective arises. This hierarchy exists regardless of one's theological tradition, political perspective, or denominational identity because, in large part, our spiritual formation has been forged in the fires of a violently capitalist and racist self-interest, even if we're part of a "progressive denomination."

Willie James Jennings, Yale professor of Africana studies and systematic theology, describes the heartbeat of white American Christianity and theological education as defined by the values of "possession," "mastery," and "control." Jennings argues that these values shape the identity of much of what passes for popular American Christianity through an image of God as one who owns and exhibits unquestioned control over the world. "White self-sufficient masculinity

is not first a person or a people," Jennings writes. "It is a way of organizing life with ideas and forming a persona that distorts identity and
strangles the possibilities of dense life together." Like social media,
this form of Christianity drains the complexity, or what Jennings calls
the "intimate and erotic energy," of shared struggle and connection in
favor of an alienated, lonely, and commodified self-sufficiency.

Since our nation's inception as a country built on the backs of
stolen labor and land, white American Christianity—that is, "folk
religion"—has often served a twofold role in the lives of middle- and
upper-middle-class white people of faith. First, it provides theological
cover for the ongoing maintenance of a divinely ordained self-interest
that has sacralized capitalist scarcity and selfishness as evidence of
God's blessing. Second, it offers a means by which those of us in power
can be absolved of our individual sins without altering the structural
realities that maintain brutality and inequality on our behalf.

The intermingling of space racialization, sacralization, and internalized capitalism is how white middle-class Southern Baptists could
excoriate Mexican Christians—many of whom were living at or below
the global poverty line—for appealing to traditional spiritualists whenever their children fell ill. Because *our* sacred spaces, *our* theology, and
our beliefs had real power behind them (not to mention an underlying
history of wealth and imperial conquest). I don't remember anyone at
the time questioning the orthodoxy of American Christians spending
close to $2 billion per year on mission excursions when roughly half
of the global population lives on less than $5.50 a day.

Traveling with my old youth choir through central Mexico opened
my eyes to the ways that not only race but access to resources so often
determines the shape, power, and scope of what passes for faithful
practice in white American Christian spaces. As a white evangelical
myself, I grew up "witnessing to" people largely because they were
poor, or brown-skinned, or didn't speak English (which, come to think
of it, sounds a lot like Jesus). Later in life, I encountered a similarly
unreflective classism among more well-heeled theological traditions
featuring robed pastors from the Ivy League, million-dollar organs,
inscrutable church polity, and a similar discomfort when people in

poverty came into the sanctuary. Capitalism, or "self-sufficient mas-culine whiteness" (as Willie James Jennings labels it), is liturgical *and* contemporary, low church *and* high church, conservative *and* progres-sive. Wherever the self-interested and self-sufficient impulse lies in the protection of your "tradition," "liturgy," "theology," "salvation," "way of life," or "historic stained glass windows," you can always tell a racist-capitalist tree by its fruit.

Rather than challenging the violently pecuniary logic of our Mar-ket God, my inherited religious tradition sought to reconcile my old youth group's growing theological and cross-cultural confusion by reaffirming the need for Christians in the majority world to assimilate to our well-funded, well-organized truth. (To be fair, we did already have matching T-shirts and permission slips.) However, the enduring "heretical" faith of these Mexican Christians introduced me to a world brimming over with questions about how certain spaces, people, and practices become sacred or profane, good or bad, resourced or ignored. When I begin giving actual thought to the God I grew up with as a white American evangelical Christian—not to mention the accompanying beliefs, causes, policies, and politicians I was expected to champion in service to this God—I dare say "folk religion" seems a terribly apt definition for what most of us were (and still are) practicing.

WHEN GOD VOTES REPUBLICAN

In 1996, as a fifth grader in my grandparents' wood-paneled den, I cried when Republican Bob Dole lost the presidential election to incum-bent Democrat Bill Clinton. My passion for the presidential aspira-tions of a then seventy-three-year-old senator from Kansas—famous for falling off the stage of a campaign rally and routinely criticizing younger, more "entitled" generations (he meant boomers!)—had very little to do with Dole's commitment to supply-side economics. Rather, my enthusiasm had very much more to do with the fact that growing up Southern Baptist in East Tennessee meant that I, as an elementary schooler who should have been playing outside or picking his nose, supported Republicans—no matter what. This makes absolutely no sense when you say it out loud. But that's the thing: no one ever did.

This is (obviously) because I was a white evangelical, a member of the Religious Right, and a "values voter"—despite not being able to vote and not knowing what any of these terms meant. Back then, I knew only that I was a Christian who went to a Southern Baptist church with his family, watched the sermons of John Hagee and Jerry Falwell on Grandma's kitchen television, and—like any *normal* person—feared the rapture and total degradation of life on earth in the days following the election of any Democrat into any public office. It wasn't so much that I loved Republicans personally but more that I respected the wishes of a God whose capricious whims, utilization of devastating weather patterns, and orchestration of terrorist activities would follow our country's refusal to vote *his* preferred candidate into office. In 1996, *that* God was a small-government Dole man—and because I wasn't terribly interested in going to hell, so was I.

In her book *The Evangelicals*, Pulitzer Prize–winning journalist Frances FitzGerald describes white evangelicals as a diverse group, incorporating, for instance, Southern Baptists, Pentecostals, and Mennonites, as well as numerous other nondenominational churches and Christian traditions with wide-ranging ecclesiastical or theological traditions. Despite the very real contextual differences between them, churches can become evangelical insofar as they center the authority, historicity, and validity of the Bible; individual salvation rooted in the saving work of Jesus Christ; the importance of evangelism; and evidence of holiness or, citing historian George Marsden, what Fitz-Gerald terms "a spiritually transformed life."

Throughout her detailed historical account of my people, FitzGerald tracks the development of the evangelical movement from its early revivalist days in the first and second Great Awakenings, through the denominational splits over slavery that characterized American Christendom during the Civil War, the ascendancy of the Religious Right as a political force in the 1980s and '90s, and the election of Donald Trump in 2016. In her treatment of white evangelicalism during Civil War and Jim Crow reconstruction, FitzGerald effectively captures the ways in which American religious institutions found themselves contextually and ideologically split apart by racist-capitalist power. These ecclesial divides over slavery between Northern and Southern congregations were further widened by a rapidly spreading economic polarization between "modernists" (in the North) and "traditionalists" (in the South) within Protestantism following the Great Depression.

Interestingly, FitzGerald understands this rift between modernists and traditionalists as rooted in each camp's response to the extreme social disparities between a desperate American workforce and the robber barons who ruled them; she writes that "modernists sought structural reform to help labor in its conflict with capital while traditionalists continued to believe that the conversion of individuals and prayer would heal the rift between the two." Princeton historian Kevin Kruse locates the ensuing political and theological debate over FDR's New Deal economic policies as inaugurating what he calls the "creation" of modern evangelicalism. That is, the modern white evangelicalism we know best was birthed by *both* a racial animus rooted in the theological protection of chattel slavery (and, later, segregation) *and* a disenfranchised corporate America struggling to rebuild its image in the aftermath of the Great Depression.

Kruse provides a compelling timeline of events that suggests that modern evangelicalism's dogged commitment to Republicanism is less a product of "values voting" on issues like abortion and marriage equality and more the dismantling of what they believed to be an overly regulated, borderline socialist New Deal apparatus. Kruse summarizes the aims of passionate midcentury clergymen: "Above all they insisted that the welfare state was not a means to implement Christ's teachings about caring for the poor and the needy, but rather a perversion of Christian doctrine. In a forceful rejection of the public service themes of the Social Gospel, they argued that the central tenet of Christianity remained the salvation of the individual. If any political and economic system fit with the religious teachings of Christ, it would have to be rooted in a similarly individualistic ethos. Nothing better exemplified such values, they insisted, than the capitalist system of free enterprise."

From the splitting of denominations over slavery during the Civil War to a radical abeyance of historically orthodox principles in the face of a reeling free market, our white American Christian tradition, like most of us, often finds itself weak-kneed in the face of power and money.

THE OPIATE OF THE MASSES

An odd-couple marriage of conservative Protestant pastors and titans of industry produced a unique cocktail of libertarian religious, economic, and political philosophy that would continue to take shape and hold a Reaganesque sway over the "hearts and minds" of the American electorate throughout the next eighty years. Kruse lays out the ways in which these politicians and powerful evangelicals utilized debates over phrases such as "One Nation Under God," "In God We Trust," and "God Bless America" in the public lexicon, as well as the introduction of state-sponsored school prayer and the appearance of the Ten Commandments in courthouses in order to repaint America's origin story as a uniquely Christian one. All of this proved particularly useful during the sociopolitical turmoil that roiled "traditional" America's self-understanding in the 1960s and 1970s as it found itself under constant threat from the insidious powers of "godless" socialism, the civil rights movement, and a growing national discontent with the Vietnam War.

In the midst of this nationwide tension, evangelical Christianity, as well as our increasingly deregulated free market economy, offered salvation to a reeling republic. Kruse highlights a particularly telling charge from Rev. Billy Graham's sermon during a crusade in Greensboro, North Carolina. In this sermon, Graham illuminated the ways that evangelical Christianity and capitalism work in concert to reveal the divinely ordained righteousness of exceedingly wealthy individuals. "[Graham] spoke at length about the 'dangers that face capitalistic America,'" Kruse writes. "If [America] hoped to survive, it needed to embrace once again 'the rugged individualism that Christ brought' to mankind. Not surprisingly, Graham saw that individualistic spirit in self-made millionaires."

Writing all the way back in 1929, Richard Niebuhr noticed the outsized role that income and social class had played in the formation of denominational identity and theology in early twentieth-century America. Within churches Niebuhr described as composed of "the disinherited" or "the poor," he found a passionate belief in a judgment day or afterlife that would promise an interruption of the power dynamics of the present. These communities often portrayed the heavenly realm as a great "reversal" of what ails and oppresses them presently. And because of this view of the afterlife, according to Niebuhr, the church of the disinherited longs for a fundamental alteration of the present order and maintains an openness toward the more radical ethical commands and teachings of Jesus.

The more radical beliefs of the churches of the disinherited stand in sharp contrast to those Niebuhr calls "the churches of the Middle Class." These churches possess an intensely personal conception of spirituality and religious practice. The churches of the Middle Class enflesh this personal spirituality through a strong emphasis on moral responsibility, self-improvement, and evidence of an ethical life, with an afterlife that maintains much of the moral and economic dynamics of the present order. For the churches of the Middle Class, one's success in achieving an ethical life (and subsequently, evidence of one's salvation) can be seen, primarily for Niebuhr, in the avoidance of poverty through the attainment of earthly occupational and financial security. Two decades earlier, Max Weber had come to similar conclusions in his foundational work *The Protestant Ethic of Capitalism*: "Restless work in a vocational calling was recommended as the best means to acquire the self-confidence that one belonged among the elect. Work, and work alone, banished religious doubt and gives certainty of one's status among the saved."

A few years ago, in my own middle-class Baptist church, a deacon delivered the following prayer just moments before passing the offering plates: "And, Lord, may we give generously in order to provide our new prospective pastor with the most important gift of all: a balanced budget." Theologian and pastor Soong-Chan Rah notes that evangelicalism has often found itself captive to the materialistic values of American society. "Typically, we will see the success of churches measured by the numerical size of the church and the financial health of the church (oftentimes reflected in the condition and appearance of the church building)," writes Rah. "Churches are no more than businesses (albeit nonprofit ones) with the bottom line being the number of attendees or the size of the church budget." When everything is for sale, white American Christianity comes rather cheaply.

From the creation of segregation academies opened under the guise of "religious freedom" across the Southeast in the 1960s and '70s as a response to federally mandated school integration to the enduring support of capital punishment and "law and order" policies from the Nixon to the Trump administrations, white American Christianity has been consistently utilized—ironically for Rev. Graham—in a rather Marxist fashion. Instead of offering a collective and creative response to the welling pain of living within a society ruled by an anxious and seemingly divinely ordained pursuit of self-interest at all costs, white American Christianity has often been an anesthetizing opiate (as Marx put it in 1843).

In language maybe more familiar to us, this kind of faith has become one more overprescribed pain pill. It diverts our collective unrest away from collaborative change and mutual understanding and into bottomless theological debate and partisan politics pretending to be denominationalism and spiritual warfare. The problem arises, though, when it seems that no matter how many culture wars you win, districts you gerrymander, or courts you pack with sympathetic judges, God's power and glory must be tenuously maintained by the tireless efforts of "his" children. Like kids of divorce, God's children anxiously understand their role in keeping the fading authority of this God and his church afloat to be a matter of life and death.

WHAT IF YOU DIED TONIGHT?

As a child, I possessed a somewhat fearful disposition toward the world. Whether it was fear of the dark, fear of dying, or fear that people would see my "weird-looking" legs (necessitating the wearing of jeans for the entirety of a sweltering summer as a body-conscious seven-year-old), there was seemingly no end to the ways in which my anxiety might frustratingly interrupt the lives of my parents. After a few years of my tearful late-night sit-ins outside my biological father and his new wife's locked bedroom door and my announcements at daycare whenever my parents pushed the envelope of the mandatory 6 p.m. pickup time that they'd forgotten me and weren't ever coming—well, my folks got desperate. Mom and Dad decided I needed Jesus *and* a therapist. I remember the therapist coloring with me, playing with Lego bricks, and kindly suggesting to my parents that I required more consistency, predictability, and empathy in the aftermath of their divorce. (I now know this is what we therapists *always* suggest.)

Much to the chagrin of my sleep-deprived mom and dad, our inherited Southern Baptist tradition took an alternative—let's say, a far more heavy metal—approach to taming my fears and anxieties: "Eric, if you were to die tonight, and all the mistakes and bad deeds of your life were played on a giant screen in front of us, do you know, based on the evidence of your life, where you would spend eternity?" And with that, as a nine-year-old struggling to navigate the inherent isolation accompanying the creation of a new family in which he possessed a different last name than all the other kids in the minivan, I was invited by a local youth speaker into a personal relationship with Jesus Christ. Unfortunately, this meant I also had to hang out with Jesus's dad a lot—who, as a "perfect heavenly Father," seemed always to be loosening his belt while shouting "You keep crying, and I'll give you something to cry about!" at most of his many children here on earth.

I discovered pretty early on in this new relationship that my heavenly Father once became so angry at me (before I was born) that he decided to kill Jesus instead of me. This, I was then told, was the *good* news. The bad news was that if I didn't accept the idea that the death of Jesus was somehow a placeholder for my own rightful termination by God for being evil since birth, then I would be killed over and over forever in a place called hell.

As you might imagine, this new personal relationship with Jesus made it even more difficult for a then fourth-grader to fall asleep or refrain from asking increasingly more anxious questions in the middle of the night. I still remember probing my groggy father in the pre-dawn light about postmortem destinations were my name to be omitted from the "lamb's book of life." He responded with—and I'm not joking—"Go read your Bible and find out" because he believed I'd fall asleep after thumbing through a few pages of my children's Bible. My biological father underestimated the bookishness of my existential angst by about three hundred illustrated pages and thirty years. I woke him up again in a few hours—and for weeks afterward.

Whether it was the apocalyptic fiction of Tim LaHaye and Jerry B. Jenkins lining the bookshelves of my childhood home or the summer camp sermons of my late adolescence and early adulthood that reminded me of just how much God's painfully violent sacrifice of his son required of me, my libido, and my weekend plans, fear and anxiety became the bread and wine (well, grape juice for us Baptists) of my childhood religious observance. For without the regular maintenance of my fundamental uneasiness in the world, I often worried that God had abandoned me altogether. Like the constant refreshing of our Twitter feeds, it was as if my sense of alienation in my own family had been co-opted—*baptized*—by my religious tradition as a sort of necessary angst keeping me in tune with the wishes of the divine and my place in "his kingdom." My capitalist American folk religion taught me that the pain was a necessary accelerant for spiritual growth, salvation, and freedom—even if it buried me in the process.

This sounds quite a bit like what the *New York Times* uncovered in their interview with our friend Jake, discussed in chapter 2: "The relentless drive to avoid [failure] seemed to come from deep inside him. He considered it a strength." Proverbs 9:10 reminds us that "the fear of the Lord is the beginning of wisdom." Speaking from experience here, just make sure you've got the right Lord keeping you awake in the middle of the night.

MORALISTIC THERAPEUTIC DEISM

In 2005, the very same year my youth choir spent a week touring through central Mexico, researchers Christian Smith and Melinda Lundquist Denton were studying the religious and spiritual lives of adolescents in the United States. In their book *Soul Searching*, Smith and Denton interpret the results of the National Study of Youth and Religion survey conducted from 2001 to 2005, and in so doing, they coin the term "Moralistic Therapeutic Deism" (MTD) as a way of better describing American adolescent faith in the early aughts. These beliefs include the following:

> God created and orders the world and watches over human life on earth.
> God wants people to be good, nice, and fair to each other, as taught in the Bible and by most world religions.
> The central goal of life is to be happy and to feel good about oneself.
> God does not need to be particularly involved in one's life except when he is needed to resolve a problem.
> Good people go to heaven when they die.

At the time Smith and Denton's findings evoked quite a bit of parental and denominational hand-wringing over the ways in which American teenagers had seemingly adopted an altogether different understanding of God than their parents. Smith and Denton's characterization of adolescent faith was often described by older adults as unhelpfully self-interested, narcissistic, and ultimately destructive for the ongoing trajectory of the church in America—except that Moralistic Therapeutic Deism wasn't unique but rather represented a further manifestation of the ways American folk religion always champions self-interest and self-sufficiency as our nation's highest moral aims.

My own initial thoughts when I first read *Soul Searching* years later as a Baptist youth pastor were "Must be nice!" As a teenager, I would have killed for a God whose central goal for my life was for me to "be happy and to feel good" about myself. Instead, I grew up thinking God killed the kid he really loved in order to begrudgingly pick me up from soccer practice and ignore me the rest of the way home. While my inherited Baptist tradition may differ markedly from the tenets outlined by Smith and Denton, there is a similar theological starting point connecting all of us across denominational traditions: *ourselves*. Self-interest—rather than beliefs about heaven, hell, or the Bible—is the unifying principle of much of what passes for American Christianity these days.

In interviews with teenagers across the denominational, sociocultural, economic, and geographic spectrum, Smith and Denton found a visible influence of Moralistic Therapeutic Deism in the personal faith statements of progressive and conservative, white and nonwhite, as well as religious and nonreligious teenagers alike. As I mentioned earlier, capitalism is progressive *and* conservative; white *and* nonwhite; high church, low church, *and* no church. The one constant theological foundation is the belief that *more* (eternal life, square footage, influence, followers, money, security) will eventually save us.

Whether manifested as a divine explanation for the continued maintenance of things as they are, a crippling fear of an uncertain future at the hands of an angry God, or a desire for divine relief from an unyieldingly oppressive life, relentless self-interest appears to be the one unifying force underneath the fraying fabric and ceaseless partisanship of our capitalist American folk religion. "Moralistic Therapeutic Deism appropriates, abstracts, and revises doctrinal elements from mostly Christianity and Judaism for its own purpose," Smith and Denton write. "But it does so in a 'downward,' apolitical direction. Its social function is not to unify and give purpose to the nation at the level of civic affairs. Rather, it functions to foster subjective well-being in its believers and to lubricate interpersonal relationships in the local public sphere. Moralistic Therapeutic Deism exists, with God's aid, to help people succeed in life."

As with everything from increased internet usage to rampant school anxiety, the seemingly self-interested faith of our teenagers does not represent an immature corrupting or degradation of the "true faith" of adults; they are instead a mirror back to ourselves. Smith and Denton conclude as much. "Few teenagers today are rejecting or reacting against the adult religion into which they are being socialized," they write. "Rather, most are living out their religious lives in very conventional and accommodating ways. The religion and spirituality of most teenagers actually strike us as very powerfully reflecting the contours, priorities, expectations, and structures of the larger adult world into which adolescents are being socialized. In many ways, religion is simply happily absorbed by youth, largely, one might say, by osmosis."

PRAISE THE LORD—OR ELSE!

"God cares more about his glory than he does about any of us," a man in ripped jeans once shouted at me and a crowd of roughly five hundred other adults and adolescents gathered for a weeklong Christian summer camp in Florida. This very loud man went on to conclude his sermon by characterizing the saving death of Jesus on the cross as that which allows God to even bear to look upon our inherent and inescapable "sinfulness." This sinfulness—this pain, really—is one we inherit from birth, the thinking goes, and spend the rest of our lives constantly managing but never really curing until we one day die and meet our maker. Like depression, our sinfulness requires regular monitoring and prevention by a God who graciously provides us the strength to continue on just as long as we keep praising, proselytizing, and proclaiming our salvation from the just punishments for our inherent brokenness. As I mentioned, I like adding the phrase "or else" to many things, not least among them the famous Christian praise chorus: "Everything that has breath, praise the Lord"—or else.

The only difference between this youth camp and all the others was that instead of paying to be there as a participant, I was being paid. As a youth pastor now, I had agency and responsibility. I was the one who voluntarily drove another air-conditioned church bus (much like the one from the Mexico trip) filled with middle-class white Baptist teenagers (much like the ones from the Mexico trip) to an experience where they would be (re)introduced to a God who is equal parts disappointed with their individual efforts at pleasing him (it's always a him) and regularly concerned with how he is being praised and perceived by them.

I remember spending the next few minutes of the sermon wondering how, exactly, any of us might ever become truly generous, humble, or self-sacrificing—like Jesus—if we remained constantly fearful of what our heavenly Father might do to us whenever we had a few questions about his parenting practices. I wondered if there would ever be a time, before death or after it, when God might finally be okay with any of us. Could this God one day actually love us independently of how we make God feel about his God-ness or his glory? I even wondered if the restlessly irritable heavenly Father I had spent a lifetime attempting to please was, like my own estranged and irritable father, never actually able to experience peace, rest, or fulfillment, no matter the number of prayers reaching his troubled ears.

What if the reason my religious fervor so often found itself incarnating this inescapable cycle of anxiety and depression within me wasn't that I was broken, sinful, or mentally unwell but that the God I had grown up with was? What if my God was as depressed and anxious as I was? How else might we describe a religion where God's power and glory are always in danger of being profaned or ultimately destroyed?

Despite its emphasis on security, ownership, and control, the God of white American Christianity is never at rest, never experiences Sabbath, never wins the struggle with satanic or secularizing forces but instead, just like our inherited, insatiable capitalism, always desires more glory, more power, more praise, and more campaign contributions. Think of white American Christianity as a pyramid scheme in danger of toppling or violating tax codes, with a God at the top of the slippery slope all of us spend our days desperately climbing and competing with one another to finally scale. We might say that because this God is never okay—is never secure in his place in our world or in our hearts—neither are we. "At church camp youth group, they're really tryin' it on us," Grace Semler Baldridge (a.k.a. Semler) mournfully intones on the track "Youth Group" for her 2021 breakthrough album *Preacher's Kid*. "Now we're grown up and we're f*&%ed up. Is there still a God we can trust?"

When I looked down the row of uncomfortable folding chairs at a group of teenagers I loved—ones battered by insatiably demanding school systems and social media feeds, as well as an internalized responsibility for success in a system where our Market God is totally comfortable sacrificing them on the altar of its ongoing flourishing—I realized the only pastoral and parental thing left to say was "Psst . . . hey, let's get the hell outta here." So we did—well, *I* did.

Three weeks after quietly ushering my old youth group out of the darkened summer camp auditorium and driving to a nearby Dairy Queen to debrief our experience, I turned in my resignation letter. Few things in life rival the oddly relieving clarity that accompanies the quitting of something that, for me, had mostly been a lifelong (and eventually professional) pursuit of trying to feel loved, worthy, and enough.

But like most triumphant mic drops, the initial endorphin spike of relief and righteous indignation soon devolves into a familiar feeling of dread and regret. I'm told this is what it's like when something (or someone) that has given your life gravity—even if that gravity felt suffocating—finally dies. As Semler works to the close of "Youth Group," she wonders about a God beyond the one she met in her old youth group: "If you're out there, I'm waitin'. If you're out there, I'm prayin'."

I found myself wondering the very same thing.

6

What If We Can't Keep Doing This?

How to Survive the Death of Your God

> In losing our faith, we may gain it back again: first faith
> ceding to second faith in the name of the stranger. . . .
> For in surrendering our own God to a stranger God no
> God may come back again. Or the God who comes
> back may come back in ways that surprise us.
>
> —Richard Kearney, *Anatheism*

In 2015, I frequently thought about killing myself. I didn't think about ending my life *every* day, just maybe a few times each week. What makes this an especially difficult confession is that 2015 was the same year my son was born. Knowing that a person whose laugh, indecipherable knock-knock jokes, and screamed *Good mornings!* are like oxygen for me entered the world at the exact same time I consistently considered leaving it—well, it is a contradictory and complex pain I struggle to name even now.

Seven years ago, when I tearfully admitted all this to my then therapist, he leaned back in his fraying armchair, closed his eyes, and quoted Jerry Seinfeld: "You kiss the baby, you love the baby. But make no mistake. Babies are here to replace us."

After what felt like an eternal pause, my old therapist quietly explained that all good parenthood is an act of gracefully being replaced by someone we love more than ourselves. He then asked me what I was in such a hurry to have my own son replace. "Everything, everything, all of this, all of me" poured out of me, like some breathy evangelical praise chorus. Then he looked me in the eyes, sat upright, and therapeutically whispered, "Eric, the best kind of dads are those willing to be replaced and willing to help the replacement happen. You could have used one of those. But now you have the chance to be one for your son."

Obviously I didn't die in 2015. Good therapy; a wife, son, and dog who love me no matter what state I find myself in; and a God I met on the other side of wanting to die—these have a way of keeping me afloat most days. That is, whenever I remember to stop trying so damn hard not to drown.

You might say that part of me did die later that year, however, because 2015 was also when I decided to quit my job as a pastor. If I'm rationalizing again, I would tell you I left the pastorate to discover what I was actually "called" to do with my life on the other side of getting paid to pray. We pastors—we're always "called." In my old job, I would argue the word *calling* functions similarly to the way the phrase "I'll pray for you" does whenever someone begins uncomfortably talking about the fullness of their pain. It effectively ends more complex and interesting questions about the world, about God, and about why exactly so many well-meaning pastors find themselves leaving smaller churches for bigger ones as an act of religious fidelity. Buddhist mystic and psychotherapist John Welwood calls this an act of "spiritual bypassing," which he describes as a "sidestepping" of "emotional issues, psychological wounds, and unfinished developmental tasks" with "spiritual ideas and practices." Spiritual bypassing is a way of using theology, God, or work to avoid or anesthetize the complicated reality of whatever pain is making unbroken eye contact with us right now.

If I'm being honest, though, I quit being a pastor for the same reasons I wanted to kill myself. After several years of internalizing the lonely pain of economic, occupational, and spiritual failure, I was burned out, anxious, and depressed. Even with so much "potential," I had turned thirty, and I found myself still desperately attempting to get my heavenly Father's attention—which should always be understood as an effort to gain increasingly larger amounts of *other* people's attention. Real professional Christians with Instagram brands and best sellers become famous by "making him famous" (points toward the heavens). In my case, the numbers didn't lie. I wasn't famous, the church where I was employed wasn't growing, and I would apparently not be making God famous anytime soon. No matter how I attempted to present myself online or at church conferences featuring sport-coated pastors complaining about being "misunderstood" by the people providing them bottomless meal per diems, I could not escape the truth. I was a small-time youth pastor at a fledgling Baptist church in East Tennessee with a new baby at home and no earthly idea what to do with my life. I left church work not because I no longer believed in God but because I no longer had faith that God believed in me.

After surveying almost 1,800 United Methodist clergy in 2013, the Clergy Health Initiative at Duke Divinity School found that when pastors were interviewed over the phone, 8.7 percent reported experiencing symptoms of depression. But when they took an anonymous web-based survey, that number jumped to 11.1 percent, which is double the national rate. The rapidly compounding nature of emotionally draining work, coupled with a professional commitment to maintaining a pastoral frame bereft of honest self-disclosure, led these researchers to note that clergy are particularly susceptible to mental health issues: "The study found that pastors' sense of guilt about not doing enough at work was a top predictor of depression, and that doubt of their call to ministry was a top predictor of anxiety. Pastors with less social support—those who reported feeling socially isolated—were at higher risk for depression." Journalist Anne Helen Petersen notes similar findings, especially in light of the compounding effects of both the pandemic and the preexisting conditions of clergy (lack of) well-being under capitalism. She found that "25% of clergy had 'seriously considered retiring or resigning' due to the stresses of performing their job during the pandemic."

Even during somewhat less apocalyptic times, I found it rather difficult as a pastor not to internalize the frustration, angst, and confusion besieging a centuries-old institution grappling with its loss of cultural power and relevancy. This was especially true when my performance reviews—from both the heavens and the poorly punctuated all-caps emails awaiting me in my in-box—screamed my professional and theological inadequacies at me in the middle of the night. *I was the problem.* Believing the growing congregational disappointment to be further confirmation of my own failure, I left the pulpit, returned to graduate school to become a psychotherapist, and because we needed the money, started working at Trader Joe's.

DO YOU WANT YOUR MILK IN A BAG?

James Baldwin once described his brief tenure as a young minister in Harlem as a kind of unmatched experience. "Nothing that has happened to me since equals the power and the glory that I sometimes felt when, in the middle of a sermon, I knew that I was somehow, by some miracle, really carrying, as they said, 'the Word'—when the church and I were one," Baldwin writes. "Their pain and their joy were mine, and mine were theirs—they surrendered their pain and joy to me."

I'm not sure what I imagined would happen when I stopped "carrying the Word" and began working at a grocery store—Baldwin would eventually write for the *New Yorker* from his home in Paris—but I can confidently say I didn't expect tendonitis to flare up in my right wrist after just seven months off the Lord's payroll. Nor did I expect its remedy to require wearing a wrist brace identifying me as someone patrons should openly pity as I struggled to put their milk in a bag. On the other hand, I was not terribly surprised by Trader Joe's customers' strong feelings about the gluten content of their potato gnocchi or by how difficult it is to steer a train of shopping carts in the driving rain while dodging SUVs piloted by moms on cell phones. Working retail grocery for the benefit of anxious white people religiously pursuing gut health is an incredibly serious business.

The hardest part of my career transition was seeing people from my old life when they came into the store. In one particularly devastating encounter, a couple whose daughter was in the bridal party of my wedding came in around Thanksgiving with a lot of questions about kosher turkeys. Upon spotting them entering through the front doors, I immediately attempted to hide behind a produce cart. But my manager soon realized I wasn't doing anything and called me over to lend a hand. The three of us chatted together about "birds" (this is how turkeys are described in the industry) for probably ten minutes. My friend's parents chose their bird, took it to the register, and went on their way. This would be totally normal except that for the entire time we talked, they had no idea it was me, Eric—someone who has definitely used their guest bathroom at least three times and was wearing a mandatory name tag that said "Eric" on it. This experience ended up foreshadowing what would become an incredibly consistent refrain during my time at the store: "Eric, is that you!? I didn't recognize you."

IT ISN'T OUR DEPRESSION THAT NEEDS INTERVENTION

When I stopped inviting rooms of Christians to close their eyes in prayer as the band made their way back onstage, it was almost as if I stopped existing altogether. Leaving something that had given my life gravity and existential heft for close to a decade felt ghostly, like I imagine entering witness protection does. Under these conditions, it's quite hard *not* to think about dying whenever you find yourself crying over a smushed peanut butter sandwich in your fifteen-year-old Civic during a thirty-minute lunch break. Avoiding "suicidal ideation" proves even more difficult whenever your thoughts turn to the six-month-old eagerly awaiting your arrival back home—a six-month-old who inevitably will eventually grow up, demand braces, and pursue an expensive degree in the humanities you can't afford.

Instead of a malfunction of brain chemistry or an inability to manifest my preferred future with positive thinking, I personally found depression to be a naturally occurring, socioemotional response to a world where economic and occupational failure was both personal and terminal. I was now a specter of sorts—a cautionary tale of what happens when you "don't go to college and have to work weekends," like one mom quietly intoned to her daughter while I bagged groceries for them on a Saturday. Incarnating this failure is like having a communicable disease in white America. Economic failure *is* moral failure around here, and it's catching—even if you, like most of my old coworkers, possess *both* a college degree and unconquerable self-respect. Maintaining this level of self-respect is difficult for retail or "essential" workers bereft of the institutional support of a company like Trader Joe's, which offers the dignity of a living wage, benefits, and a retirement plan (even if they make you call your manager "Captain").

EVEN DISILLUSIONMENT IS A FORM OF PRIVILEGE

Clearly, my "failure" as an overly educated white guy in America was always relative. Many of my peers, especially those from traditionally marginalized or underresourced communities, would have been grateful to have a steady job and a baby boy at home. To become disillusioned with this kind of life, one must first have been living with other illusions. Midlife (or even quarter-life) crises are an example of an odd form of privilege white Americans enjoy that doesn't exist for many people of color. Toward the end of his life, James Baldwin sharply diagnosed the relative absence of just these kinds of existential crises in his own Black community as rooted in a well-earned doubt in the fundamental goodness of the American dream:

The American Negro has the great advantage of having never believed the collection of myths to which white Americans cling: that their ancestors were all freedom-loving heroes, that they were born in the greatest country the world has ever seen, or that Americans are invincible in battle and wise in peace. . . . Negroes know far more about white Americans than that; it can almost be said, in fact, that they know about white Americans what parents—or, anyway, mothers—know about their children, and that they very often regard white Americans that way. And perhaps this attitude, held in spite of what they know and have endured, helps to explain why Negroes, on the whole, and until lately, have allowed themselves to feel so little hatred. The tendency has really been, insofar as this was possible, to dismiss white people as the slightly mad victims of their own brainwashing.

Few terms so aptly encapsulate what has happened to us anxiously fearful white Americans as "brainwashing." Anytime our minds, souls, and bodies rebel against the inhumane treatment we endure (and exact on others) in our pursuit of an increasingly out-of-reach happiness, they are quickly bypassed by diagnoses, substances, or a religiously mandated internalization of our pain as some sort of biological failure or moral inadequacy.

As Baldwin attests, the angst besieging my own and subsequent generations of "slightly mad" white Americans is a counterintuitive component of the privilege we enjoy as citizens still able to believe that this system might one day benefit us. This fiction has never been afforded to the people of color whose land, labor, and lives were seen as the unfortunate sacrifices for the flourishing of our ever-expanding nation. I was raised to believe that the systemic inequalities disproportionately impacting communities of color were the necessary evils of living in an overly complicated world and, as such, could remain contained therein. Institutional racism is yet one more form white America's compartmentalized pain, fear, and scarcity takes.

This angst has begun wafting, however—like the smell of sewage when the wind changes—into the schools and communities of white America's middle and upper-middle class. We are thus presented with a choice: either continue internalizing our market-driven anxiety and depression as further evidence of our personal failures in an increasingly unequal society or begin collectively resisting an American life where our salvation has been rebranded into a frenetic lust for security. On the other side of our growing mental health crisis, we can either continue accepting or begin resisting a life in which we are mandated to kill or be killed, eat or be eaten, or sacrifice or be sacrificed on an altar of divinely ordained self-interest.

In his landmark work on the development of racist ideas *Stamped from the Beginning*, Ibram X. Kendi argues that self-interest serves as the seedbed of our institutionally racist policies and practices: "These many forms of [antiracist] educational persuasion, like uplift suasion, have been predicated on the false construction of the race problem: the idea that ignorance and hate lead to racist ideas, which lead us to racist policies. In fact, self-interest leads to racist policies, which lead to racist ideas leading to all the ignorance and hate. Racist policies were created out of self-interest." This is another way of describing exactly how market competition undermines our relational, political, spiritual, and economic well-being to the point of sorting and dividing us so thoroughly we can no longer collectively resist its spread.

Despite the claims of politicians who actively hate a government they desperately campaign to work for every few years, self-interest won't ever save our country, our economy, our churches, our children, or us. As I said much earlier, anxious self-improvement and violent self-interest are what capitalism looks like when it has been religiously internalized. This is because our individual efforts at self-improvement occur within a larger system that actively profits off our isolation and competition. So our actual liberation can only lie entangled with the fate of those whom we have rejected, avoided, competed with, ignored, judged, imprisoned, and sometimes even crucified. As Indigenous Australian artist, activist, and academic Lilla Watson famously reminded the United Nations during its 1985 Decade for Women Conference in Nairobi, "If you have come here to help me, you are wasting your time. But if you have come because your liberation is bound up with mine, then let us work together."

EYES REMADE FOR WONDER

One cold Sunday night in February, I found myself impatiently waiting for the last dregs of the grocery store to make their way to the front with their final purchases. If you haven't worked retail grocery, let me be clear: Sunday-night shoppers have a lot going on. As folks slowly began queuing up at the registers a little bit before 9 p.m., a woman in sunglasses, a large head wrap, and a neck bandage rattled up to my line with what looked like an entire grocery cart filled with cranberry juice. "Great," I thought, "another Sunday-night shopper." I opened our transaction with an old retail standby: "So how are you tonight, Ma'am?" Her response (without looking up): "Fine." Off to a good start.

If you've ever been to Trader Joe's, you know that during checkout, employees effusively praise at least one item in your cart as a way of generating human connection. My options were severely limited by the contents of this shopper's grocery haul, so I opted for a half-hearted if also gently sarcastic "I see you are enjoying our cranberry juice." Her response (still not looking up): "It's the only thing that will settle my stomach after chemotherapy."

Almost every day, we encounter moments in which throwaway comments or lowered gazes invite us to slow down, take a deep breath, and authentically enter into the pain of someone else. Typically, we ignore these few minutes amid the noise, clutter, and ceaseless doom scroll of existence—an existence in which our inherited predisposition toward scarcity and self-interest has a way of teaching all of us that there's never enough of anything to go around. The thought, then, of pausing to take on more from someone else doesn't just seem overwhelming; it seems fundamentally wrongheaded and self-destructive. When we are so rarely okay, there is never enough in the tank for anything but, as Margaret Thatcher prophesied, the survival of your-self and your family, "society" be damned.

Yet for some unknown and possibly miraculous reason, at the end of a long shift when I found myself particularly angry about quitting a cushy church job where I wasn't paid by the hour to make small talk about cranberry juice, I meagerly offered, "I'm sorry to hear that. How has it been going?" This olive branch was immediately snapped in two by the woman's gruff announcement that she was "dying from the cancer that has already claimed my adult son—so, not well, I guess you could say."

(And all God's people said, "Ahhhh, shit. This is why you just say, 'I'm fine' all the time.")

My manager (a.k.a. "Captain"), Tony, tirelessly encouraged all of us on staff to give things away to customers whenever the moment presented itself to us, no questions asked. He was, to this day, the best boss I ever had, and I once worked for the Lord. So as the line built up behind her, I locked my register, excused myself, walked over to our almost-empty fresh flower bin, and chose one of the last remaining bouquets of (probably wilted) flowers. Upon my return, dripping flowers in tow, I mustered, "Well, I don't have much to offer, except to say that these are pretty much the last $5.99 flowers left in the store, and I want you to have them, on the house."

When she looked up for the first time, her breath caught in her throat, and through tears, she choked out, "Eric, huh? That was my son's name."

And right there, in a soon-closing Trader Joe's overlooking Inter-state 40, I started crying and hugging a complete stranger while a line of six other people waited behind us—which reminds me of how Rabbi Lawrence Kushner once described the true purpose of religion as returning us to wherever we are "with eyes remade for wonder."

THE GOD WHO SEES

In John's Gospel, we happen upon a scene featuring several of Jesus's closest followers cowering in a room "with the doors locked for fear of the Jewish leaders" (John 20:19 NIV); this is just days after his untimely death at the hands of the Roman Empire. These earliest disciples are painfully aware that Jesus isn't the first religious revolutionary amassing a following and an untimely death at the hands of occupying authorities. Suffice it to say that when the government kills your God, it makes excellent sense to hide like bandits on the edge of town. So they do.

Amid tension, fear, and abandonment, the author of John's Gospel tells us that the resurrected Jesus mysteriously shows up, even though the door is locked: "Jesus came and stood among them and said, 'Peace be with you!' After he said this, he showed them his hands and side" (20:19–20 NIV). Unfortunately, one of the disciples, Thomas, who has presumably been out getting groceries, missed this mystical encounter with his recently risen Lord. Upon hearing the stammered accounts of his friends about Jesus's scar-bearing, peace-giving arrival, Thomas naturally remains a bit skeptical, even going so far as to claim that it would take sticking his fingers in the nail holes to believe what the other disciples were telling him about the resurrected Christ. A week later Thomas finds his skepticism rewarded, as the resurrected Jesus appears for a second time, "though the doors were [still] locked" (20:26 NIV).

Growing up, I was strongly encouraged to pay close attention to the way Jesus chides Thomas for his lack of faith and for believing in him only "because he had seen" and not in the absence of sight like later believers, whose sightless faith would find itself "blessed" (John 20:29). This concluding sentence was supposed to be an authorial encouragement or "blessing" to those of us reading and believing this story years later in the absence of the physical evidence of resurrection. Instead of relief, though, I soon found myself buried under the pressure to keep believing in a God whose peace seemed always just out of reach, off stage, or in some disembodied future home upon my death.

Like Thomas, I wanted nothing but to desperately stick my hands in the scars and nail holes of my dead God.

Back behind the register at Trader Joe's, I found that my own once sure, professional faith had been dashed on the rocks of an unshakable depression as well as a crippling fear that I was actually alone in the world and had been for some time now. The God I had put my faith, hope, and trust in had died at the hands of another global empire hell-bent on profit and conquest at all costs. And in the wake of this God's death, I was angry, I was hopeless, and I was incredibly worried that admitting all this out loud had destroyed not only my own but my entire family's future. More than once I thought, "I should have hidden my pain and kept taking the money and good health insurance because that's what real adults do."

Yet I found myself face-to-face with the resurrected Jesus anyway. Except that this time, instead of being a crucified Jewish man in his early thirties, he wasn't a man at all. This Jesus didn't immediately demand to know why my faith had failed to adequately reflect his unending glory. The Jesus I met at Trader Joe's wasn't triumphant; she was dying. She wasn't angry but tired. And she wasn't overly concerned with how many people were backing up behind her in line. The Jesus I met in the middle of a closing shift introduced me to a world and a God beyond perfection, beyond self-interest, beyond self-sufficiency, and beyond scarcity. This God saved my life.

"Eric, huh? That was my son's name" became an unexpected opportunity to return to the truth of who all of us actually are underneath all the branding and bullshit: complicated humans with names, stories, pains, and triumphs. The act of two strangers slowing down long enough to authentically bear witness to one another's pain—in a crowded grocery store at the end of an incredibly long day—brought the kind of understanding and deep knowing that I had sought for most of my life. This deep knowing didn't come at the end of all my hard work but in the midst of my loneliness and "failure." As Hagar reminds us in the book of Genesis after being kicked out of Abraham's house with a new baby and no future, "You are the God who sees me" (16:13 NIV).

Even though I had imploded my life, and none of it had found itself put back together just yet, and even though the woman across from me was dying from a cancer that had already claimed her son, we saw each other. In so doing, we were okay for a while. And if two strangers in line can be okay for a while together, sitting in the warm glow of our shared complexity as flesh-and-blood humans instead of "grocery clerk" and "cancer patient," I wonder what else the rest of us could be, together?

BUT WHAT IF WE WERE OKAY?

It is particularly unexpected for Americans to meet a God who willingly enters into locked rooms (or grocery stores) with bald head wrapped, scarred hands open, scarred sides bared, and only one request: for peace to be with us. This is because we have been taught to view any invitation for peace, well-being, or salvation that doesn't come with an expenditure of money or hard work from us as a scam. As this thinking in my own inherited faith tradition goes, "God first loves and forgives us; that's what grace is about. But if you have a hard time believing in that, God will also send you to hell. See you on Sunday!" What if the reason we find ourselves so isolated from the God I met in the grocery store is due not to this God's increasingly noticeable absence but to our own inability to pause long enough from our frenetic efforts at surviving to realize that peace and okayness have been with us the whole time? We just didn't recognize them.

Boston College professor of philosophy Richard Kearney advocates for what he calls the reclamation of "God after God." He suggests that "first faith cedes to second faith" as people release the gods they grew up with in the face of pain, loss, or dislocation. Whatever God returns to us on the other side of our first God's death becomes a "stranger God," Kearney says, because it is one whose presence greets us in ways "that may surprise us."

What could be more surprising (and saving) than the good news that peace is already with us and has been the whole time? This peace doesn't come for us at the end of a contentious election, after a life spent toiling for retirement, or after we've finally done enough to fill the Market God–shaped hole inside all of us. Instead, it greets us right in the midst of our crippling disappointment and catastrophic fear. At *that* moment—before the triumphant "getting better" movie montage—what if we were okay? What if we were loved? What if we could float?

And what if this kind of God—one dripping with a radical kind of okayness and one utterly devoid of self-interest—could unlock the door to all sorts of possibilities beyond the anxious, burned-out, and fearful life many of us have been living? I have begun believing this kind of life on the other side of the Market God's death is available to us if only we unlock the door. Even if we don't, though, radical okayness just might come for us anyway.

The rest of this book is about that kind of God and about that kind of okayness.

What If We Weren't Afraid of Our Feelings?

How to Listen to Our Pain as an Act of Resistance

Anger is a catalyst. Holding on to it will make us exhausted and sick. Internalizing anger will take away our joy and spirit; externalizing anger will make us less effective in our attempts to create change and forge connection. It's an emotion that we need to transform into something life-giving: courage, love, change, compassion, justice. Or sometimes anger can mask a far more difficult emotion like grief, regret, or shame, and we need to use it to dig into what we're really feeling. Either way, anger is a powerful catalyst but a life-sucking companion.

—Brené Brown, *Braving the Wilderness*

Several years ago I found myself deep in conversation with a man I'd just met. This kind of thing happens to therapists a lot—except this time my conversation partner wasn't a patient, and I wasn't in my office; I was in someone else's backyard.

After breaking the ice with a rather perfunctory "So, what do you do for a living?" my new friend off-handedly mentioned that he once worked in management for a major US retailer. "Pardon my French," he conspiratorially nudged me, "but I was damn good at my job, and if not for physically stopping a shoplifter from leaving the store I would probably still work there."

What was interesting about this stranger's sudden confession about his old job was that before leaving the company, he made clear that he would always stick up for his employer—their work in the community and the good they do across the world. And then they fired him. After this, he told me, it took about eight weeks before he woke up to the realization that what he had been doing—cutting peoples' hours, declining requests for health insurance, initiating layoffs, as well as carrying out other practices demanded by his bosses— was completely unethical. My new friend told me that some of his bosses took home bonuses larger than the yearly salaries of the people he was laying off. The bonuses actually got bigger the more he slashed.

What he said next still sticks with me: "Eric, I'm not religious. But it was like I was possessed by something. It took getting fired to wake me up to it."

As a thoroughly modern person, you would think talking about something weird like demon possession in mixed company would be a bit uncomfortable. But I struggle to find a better term for what it's like to hear parents scream at their children in semipro youth league sports for not hustling enough, watch teenagers come to blows because they've had their brands stolen, hear my first grader describe his participation in active-shooter drills at school, or watch retirees try to sign up for Medicare. For many of us, this kind of life is normal. Yet when we stop and say it out loud, a question arises: "Wait, what?"

I mentioned in the last chapter that James Baldwin likens the kind of possession my neighbor is describing to a form of "brainwashing." This brainwashing deludes many of us Americans into believing that the Market God we evangelically praise and refuse to doubt will one day reward our faithfulness. Until, that is, we become a bad investment, or complicated, or tired, or burned out, or no longer useful for this God's ongoing, eternal growth. So we judiciously hide our fears, our imperfections, our doubts, our struggles, and our deep pain from the God we've grown up with, from others, and even from ourselves. Because if we don't, there will be hell to pay.

This system—religion, really—teaches us that our pain and confusion in the face of what passes for modern life are a sign of weakness and will eventually interrupt or wreck our futures. The pain is mandatory and so is our silence. My new friend and I, however, had found that peace and truth have a way of floating to the surface anyway—most especially in the midst of our grief over the sudden loss of everything we thought would one day save us. Rather than killing us, listening to and airing our deep pain freed us both to return to ourselves, to our families, and to our community with a newfound sense of wonder and possibility.

To get there, though, we must be willing to listen to our pain, to look it in the eye, and to call it by name.

"WHAT IS YOUR NAME?"

In the fifth chapter of Mark's Gospel, we come across an encounter featuring Jesus, a bloodied and shrieking demon-possessed man living among the tombs on the outskirts of his town, and a herd of drowned pigs. The Bible may be a lot of unhelpful things to a lot of people, but it's almost never boring.

In this story, Jesus and his disciples have sailed across the Sea of Galilee and landed in a region identified as "the country of the Gerasenes." Mark tells us that "immediately" after exiting their boat, Jesus and the disciples are greeted by "a man out of the tombs with an unclean spirit," who "lived among the tombs; and no one could restrain him any more, even with a chain; for he had often been restrained with shackles and chains, but the chains he wrenched apart, and the shackles he broke in pieces; and no one had the strength to subdue him. Night and day among the tombs and on the mountains he was always howling and bruising himself with stones" (Mark 5:1–5). Welcome to Gerasene!

After running to Jesus and bowing down before him, the demon-possessed man requests that Jesus "not torment" him. The text tells us that this request is connected to an earlier demand from Jesus that the unclean spirits "come out of" the man. Before going any further, however, Jesus pauses to ask the man his name. "Legion," the demons reply and soon ask "not to be sent out of the country" but instead to enter into the nearby herd of swine. Jesus relents and the demons possess the herd of pigs, which promptly rushes down a steep embankment to drown in the nearby sea. I wasn't lying when I told you the Bible isn't boring.

In response, the shocked swineherds run back into town, presumably to let everyone know they aren't responsible for the death of two thousand pigs (not to mention a great deal of lost profit): "Then people came to see what it was that had happened. They came to Jesus and saw the demoniac sitting there, clothed and in his right mind, the very man who had had the legion; and they were afraid. . . . Then they began to beg Jesus to leave their neighborhood" (Mark 5:14–15, 17). What does it say about the Gerasenes that the only time they're "afraid" is when the formerly shrieking and bleeding man chained up in the cemetery outside town is "clothed and in his right mind"?

Stanford historian René Girard, in his book *The Scapegoat*, argues that one of the most frightening things for the Gerasenes in this encounter isn't the presence of a man possessed but the sudden *absence* of a scapegoat. Once they no longer have a problem upon which they can lay their angst, fear, violence, and pain, chaos ensues. "A symmetry can be seen," Girard opines, "in all these extremes, the self-laceration and the running among the tombs on the one hand, the grandiloquent chains on the other. There is a sort of conspiracy between the victim and his torturers to keep the balance in the game because it is so obviously necessary to keep the balance of the Gerasene community." In my training as a marriage and family therapist, we would call this becoming the "problem" for the sake of the family system. Becoming a "problem" is not a job we choose for ourselves or even one someone chooses for us; it's something that happens to us. To wake up to it—to come alive to the water in which we've been swimming—we need an experience with someone willing to empathically ask us our name and about what raised us—even if we come shrieking at them out of some nearby tombs.

Whenever therapists, pastors, parents, teachers, regular people, or even the Son of God interrupts the way things normally function, the system enters a state of panic because it no longer knows where to find the problem. Luo Huazhong found this out firsthand when he kicked off a countercultural movement among Chinese millennials with a blog post entitled "Lying Flat Is Justice."

"Lying flat" (or *tangping* in Mandarin) is, according to Elsie Chen in her piece for the *New York Times* on the phenomenon, "to forgo marriage, not have children, stay unemployed and eschew material wants such as a house or a car. It is the opposite of what China's leaders have asked of their people." Chen interviews another Chinese millennial, Leon Ding, who dropped out of his college computer science program and refuses to participate in a "996" Chinese work culture typically characterized by an expectation that employees will work 9 a.m. to 9 p.m. six days a week. "I want a stable job that allows me to relax," Ding says, "but where can I find it?" In response to the growing numbers of Chinese millennials lying flat, the ruling Communist Party has outlawed the practice as a form of social instability and continues to censor, delete, and remove references to it online and throughout the country. "Those people who say lying down is shameful are shameless. I have the right to choose a slow lifestyle," Luo Huazhong argues. "I didn't do anything destructive to society. Do we have to work 12 hours a day in a sweatshop, and is that justice?"

From families to the global economy, the absence of a clearly defined problem is terrifying to every system. No matter their size, these systems will do anything within their power to maintain homeostasis—which usually means asking the one interrupting them to leave or get back to work.

In the case of the Gerasenes, it is cheaper, easier, and more comfortable to let someone who is screaming and cutting himself sleep outside than it is to figure out how much it's going to cost for all of them to heal a culture that produces this kind of person. In the case of the global economy, it's much easier to hang up nets outside sweatshop factories to catch the bodies of workers attempting to end their lives than to question the needs of an insatiable free market desperate for cheap labor. In the case of much of the work I did at a high school, it was cheaper, easier, and more comfortable for the system to let "problem" students sleep outside, screaming and cutting themselves, than it was to figure out how much it was going to cost for them to be clothed, sitting in class, and in their right minds.

In this kind of world, both then and now, my man Legion is the only one telling the truth.

When we slow down, we quickly discover that the humans before us are constantly fascinating and instructive and miraculous. They have names and shaping experiences and one day could become, if our imaginations will allow it, clothed and in their right minds.

When I choose to believe that the true God of the universe is one who, when meeting a screaming and self-harming man on the outskirts of town, leans forward, looks him in the eye, and asks him his name, *it changes everything*. I know this because when the true God of the universe interrupted my closing shift and made unbroken eye contact with my pain and feelings of profound failure, it changed everything for me. It changed how I began understanding why I was so profoundly sad and anxious. It changed how I interact with those I have so quickly and thoroughly shackled away as "crazy" or "monstrous" on the outskirts of my own sociopolitical community. It changed the way I read the Bible and think about my son. It changed my job and my past and my future. It set my feet, as the old hymn goes, on solid ground.

Meeting this God gave me a way of returning to a world crumbling around me with a kind of open-handed, radical okayness that might not immediately save or fix anything but my ability to be fully myself, without apology, for maybe the very first time.

"What's your name?" is a question that has all sorts of resurrecting possibilities attached to it. I've found that once people stop being "them"—once they stop being statistics, diagnoses, problems, or useful for the maintenance of an inhumane system—and start being flesh-and-blood humans made up of both good and bad experiences that have profoundly shaped who they are, they quickly start becoming themselves again. And it's amazing how quickly I do as well. Listening to our pain can be revolutionary if we'll let it. But the letting it? Well, that's the hard part.

"I DON'T EVEN LIKE MY FEELINGS!"

Once, when my son was three, I found him attempting to cram large plastic dinosaurs into glasses full of water on our dining room table. Rather quickly—with movements not seen since my days playing basketball for my completely defeated middle school team—I angrily snatched the dinosaurs out of his hands and threw them to the ground, all with parental impunity. As you might imagine, this move resulted in a tantrum of earsplitting, volcanic toddler rage.

Luckily, because I am a very good therapist, I told my thrashing toddler of a son that for the duration of his meltdown, I would be retiring to the living room—where, upon calming down, he was welcome to join me for a thoughtful discussion about his very valid feelings regarding the "thirsty" dinosaurs I "stole" from him. (For the record, he did not, instead choosing to register his discontent by shouting from the adjoining dining room, *I'm not talking about my feelings. I don't even like my feelings!*")

Being the only child of two therapists is almost certainly a dream scenario for any kid, and that fact is (I'm assuming) the underlying subtext of my boy's earsplitting elegy. To be fair to my son, though, no one else seems to care all that much for their feelings these days, especially the difficult, ambivalent, or troubling ones. To understand this phenomenon, though, and the powerful role that listening to our pain plays in resurrecting unconsidered possibilities for the world around us, we must first deal with why exactly our pain has been so effectively buried in the first place.

SO HOW ARE YOU?

In an interview for the *Atlantic*, psychologist, author, and founder of the Emotional Intelligence Skills Group David Caruso notes the ways in which our uniquely American approach to conversation around emotion fundamentally limits our ability to tell one another the truth of what's actually happening inside and around us. Beginning with our collective use of the phrase "How are you?" as a common greeting, Caruso argues that answering most open-ended, feelings-based questions in America with anything other than "great" can be an incredibly fraught experience: "American culture demands that the answer to the question 'How are you?' is not just 'Good,' but sometimes 'Great.' Or—this drives folks around the world crazy, who might be based in another country but they work for an American company—we need to be 'Awesome.' There's this relentless drive to mask the expression of our true underlying feelings. It's almost inappropriate."

In her award-winning novel *Americanah*, Chimamanda Ngozi Adichie notices a similar cultural demand for awesomeness. Even in "progressive circles," minority and immigrant communities are expected to emotionally whitewash (pun intended) their experiences of racism, misogyny, and the collective pain of living under a profoundly untrue narrative of meritocracy. Or as Adichie's protagonist, Ifemelu, rants to her fellow progressive guests at a tony Manhattan dinner party following the DNC's confirmation of Obama's candidacy for president, "The only reason you say that race was not an issue is because you wish it was not. We all wish it was not. But it's a lie. . . . We don't talk about [our pain]. . . . We say that race doesn't matter because that's what we're supposed to say, to keep our nice liberal friends comfortable. It's true. I speak from experience."

Failing to authentically tell ourselves and others the truth about the pain we are experiencing alienates us from one another; if left to fester, it will eventually destroy us. Perhaps what we are seeing amid increasing political polarization and violence in America isn't just partisanship but a severe symptom of our increasingly desperate desire for authentic connection. Perhaps our cultlike political identities are an effort to decrease the profound hopelessness, isolation, and anger we so often feel as Americans.

Caruso argues that one possible source of this nationwide disconnection is our discomfort with expressing more difficult personal emotions in public: "Really good quality long-term interpersonal relationships are based on shared experience but also the ability to share how we are feeling at that time. . . . If you are always expected to say 'great,' you're never going to have that level of intimacy that you need in a really good relationship."

University of Toronto psychologist Brett Ford essentially echoes Caruso's sentiments in her 2018 study investigating the health benefits of "accepting negative emotions." In a sample of 1,300 adults, Ford found that people who "tend not to judge their feelings" or "not think about their emotions as good or bad" typically possess "better" mental well-being across numerous measures. This is due, she argues, to our frequently anxious efforts at willing ourselves to become happier, as well as our reflexive shame at feeling bad. The cyclical relationship between our anxious efforts at being awesome and the emotional drain of our shame at not pulling it off ends up producing the confounding emergence of what Ford terms "meta-emotions." Metaemotions are characterized by the rise of judgmental feelings, like disappointment, about our own "not-awesome" inner emotional turmoil. Over time, Ford notes that these feelings can "accumulate" and ultimately "damage" our mental health.

Metaemotion is depression about being depressed, anxiety about being anxious, and frustration that we can't seem to get ourselves together even though everyone on Instagram seems to be doing awesomely. Think of metaemotions as internalized invalidations of whatever you are experiencing in response to the world around you. What makes metaemotion so difficult to talk about directly is that it often appears as thoughtful, logical, or even well-reasoned responses to our pain. For instance, before my psychotherapy patients describe mistreatment, abuse, or abandonment, they often begin with a few introductory remarks about how "I know this might sound dumb" or "I know people all across the globe are struggling, but . . ." Metaemotion is what it feels like to rebrand our naturally occurring responses to the trickle-down pain of American life as less the responsibility of a system that has harmed us and more the result of our own failure to cope and perform under any condition.

Saying the quiet part out loud—about the cultural expectation of a default American "awesomeness"—helps us uncover the ways in which our conversations both with friends and with ourselves remain fundamentally inauthentic. Militant awesomeness is a brand we're taught to cultivate, and despite the fact that we know we're lying, this brand of awesomeness eventually alienates us and destabilizes us to the point that we can no longer tell fact from fiction, demagoguery from democracy, friend from foe, joy from sadness.

This happens not because our pain is inappropriate or even wrong-headed; it's because our world demands that our pain be transformed into a happily productive or consumptive activity providing momentary relief, not to mention ongoing economic growth. American capitalism—or what I've begun calling the anxious pursuit of salvation at all costs—is a long-standing grift. It promises us that if we ignore our present pain and the pain of those around us for long enough, then we will eventually be rewarded in the future with a feeling that has eluded us since we were born: *enough*.

YOUR CAPITALISM HAS BEEN INTERNALIZED

Over the past several chapters, I have attempted to make plain the ways in which the enshrinement of ceaseless competition and hyperventilating excess drive increasingly destructive economic and social policy here in America. While this desire for bottomless growth directly erodes our social safety nets, educational policy, and democracy, it also trickles down to the level of our individual conceptions of self-worth, morality, religion, and meaning. When this happens, our capitalism becomes something more than mere economic policy; it becomes fully catechized, or internalized. Internalized capitalism fundamentally unbalances us and knocks our sense of self off course. It removes our ability to authentically describe the kind of pain we are experiencing for fear that we will eventually pay for our lack of faith in the market's wisdom. So we just keep working.

Much like what our friend Legion discovered in Gerasene some two thousand years ago, this kind of self-interested system ends up passively teaching all of us to doubt what we're hearing and seeing (like a man screaming in the cemetery, for instance), and it directly impacts the amount of freedom we can feel in our relationships with one another. If this seems overblown, think of the ways larger structural and environmental factors shape our understanding of what is a "normal" or even "right" response to the moment in front of us—whether that moment be on Twitter amid a contentious election season or in the first few seconds after the doors slide open at the Target near your house on Black Friday. "Normal" and "right" are almost always contextually determined. It takes a superhuman effort to muster something resembling compassion, depth, and a nuanced appreciation of human complexity whenever we'd like our tweet to go viral or when there are only one hundred televisions available at the advertised price.

Within a structure defined by constant competition, a "normal" response is to shy away from any display of doubt, weakness, or pain in the presence of other competitors against whom we struggle for increasingly scarce resources. This kind of winner-take-all response to scarcity is why it's hard to make trustworthy friends as a middle schooler or have complicated discussions about politics as an adult. Fear of failure ramps up anxiety in our relationships, activates our physiological responses to danger, and decreases our propensity for empathy, creativity, or complex reasoning. To protect us from harm or vulnerability, the body bypasses the parts of the brain that might cause us to slow down in the midst of stress because it is worried something bad will happen. As a general rule, we don't enjoy being vulnerable around our competitors—even those we call friends. This might help to explain why many of our relationships now feel so thoroughly empty and almost wholly transactional in nature even after we finish eighth grade.

Maintaining authentic human connection amid twenty-first-century scarcity and competition feels similar to what making friends with strangers in the opening moments of a Black Friday sale might be like. If we pause in conversation for too long, the things we want will sell out. If we stop clawing and competing, we will be left with nothing. If we don't update our kitchen like our friends just did, we are reminded of just how behind or in debt we are or how far we have still to climb. And if we don't push our kids and ourselves hard enough, all of us drown.

Endless competition and comparison uproot us and remove our feet from solid ground. These feelings are not unlike shakily standing on one foot, and when we fear that we might fall, the range of creative responses to the Black Friday sale we've started calling "life" becomes incredibly limited. In my work as a therapist, these responses typically look like anxiety and anger on the one hand or withdrawal and depression on the other. Either way, they reflect a state of reactive hopelessness and helplessness that leaves us the lonely victims of a world out of control.

Whenever these painful jolts of authenticity push up through the crust of our curated fakeness, a friend is likely to gently suggest that we "talk to someone"—as in someone *else*, because our pain is now expressing itself in a decidedly unpopular and altogether uncomfortable way for a world demanding unyielding awesomeness. Frustratingly, whenever these expressed feelings no longer match what Bruce Rogers-Vaughn calls "the expected mood," they are often pathologized, medicated, and silenced by a mental health field ruled by the same market forces that brought us to treatment in the first place.

Even at the end of a successful round of psychotherapy, we likely characterize our "problem" as an individual failure of cognition or biology, with language describing how we were depressed, anxious, or overmedicating with food, television, booze, or work. To be fair to us therapists, it's hard to get health insurance to cover the naturally occurring pain of living in a society where self-worth is constantly tethered to how much we produce and what the market believes that production is worth. Most mental health providers—and educators, retail managers, politicians, clergy, and even Silicon Valley executives—aren't expressly nefarious or exploitative. Instead, all of us find ourselves structurally "possessed" by what Walter Wink terms "the Powers that Be" or "domination systems": systems in which individual goodwill, morality, and ethical decision-making by those "in charge" are quickly undermined by larger systemic rules. In this kind of system, Wink argues, "Managers are, in fact, more or less interchangeable. Most people in managerial positions would tend to make the same sorts of moves. A great many of their decisions are being made for them by the logic of the market, the pressures of competition, and/or the cost of workers." I think my new friend who found himself "possessed" by the values of an out-of-control retail industry would agree—which begs the question, If all this is too big to change, what hope is left?

Much like those indiscriminately shocked dogs from psychologist Martin Seligman's famous study of learned helplessness, we can find it difficult to stay politically and socially engaged when it feels like our only options are indiscriminate rage or exhausted disconnection. Theologian and professor of philosophy Cornel West terms this kind of experience a "deadening nihilism," defined by "psychic depression, personal worthlessness, and social despair" where hope is eliminated by "a market morality that undermines a sense of meaning and larger purpose."

When we feel helpless and unbalanced, our so-called "negative" feelings are often the only ones telling us the truth about that helplessness. To hear that your pain must be attended to, treated respectfully, and given a full hearing rather than being immediately ignored can feel as self-destructive as being told to roll over and float on your back when you feel like you might drown. It's hard to trust that airing the truth of what we've all been going through won't pull us further under the water. This is why we have to (re)learn how to truly grieve.

THE RECOVERY OF GRIEF

Early in my pastoral career, I met a woman who had recently lost a child during pregnancy due to a serious car accident. In the midst of her quiet witness to the sudden death of her unborn child, I responded with what I believed to be a heartfelt "I'm so sorry." Upon hearing me, she immediately looked up and gravely intoned, "Oh honey, I'm not. My parents had been out of church for years, and now my baby's death has brought them back to the Lord. *This was all part of his plan.*"

While I had heard about this God's plan before, I had yet to meet quite so happy a victim of it. One of the reasons I became a pastor in the first place was that at age thirteen, I met my own youth pastor, Kal. He lived next door to my grandparents and, much to my grandfather's chagrin, always cut their shared hedgerow "way too short." Kal had worked at my childhood Baptist church for over twenty years by the time I entered the youth group. Before this point, I had only attended church against my will. That all changed the first time a seemingly eight-foot-tall, incredibly tan, and mischievous Floridian gave "his testimony" about selling drugs behind the auto parts store where he worked in college. Kal had seen some things.

After a few years of watching him gleefully hit kids with dodge balls, preach sermons in front of gray-faced adults where us kids would dare him to say words we all agreed upon ahead of time, and maintain this unrelenting interest in people the rest of the church seemed to just sort of tolerate, I began telling Kal about what it was like to grow up in my family. And instead of inviting me to reflect upon my sinfulness or the powerful surety of God's great plan in the face of my teenage angst, Kal just kept agreeing with me and crying alongside me. He never defended God or my parents, and he never became uncomfortable with my pain; he just quietly acknowledged that he had it too. His pain had yet to destroy him, and because of that, I began slowly believing mine might not destroy me either.

Instead of inviting me to become a Christian by bypassing my doubt and confusion with some sort of prayer or confirmation class, Kal showed me what it was like to be a person who believes in God but also sometimes has to call God on his shit whenever it feels like God has forgotten us.

Only upon becoming a therapist some years later would I begin understanding that the difficulty of any healing profession isn't found in grappling with the trauma and grief inherent in the uncovering of an individual's, couple's, or family's pain. Rather, the true challenge for therapists, pastors, chaplains, and counselors is to hold someone, without judgment, in the presence of their own grief—and to hold them there long enough to let the grief and pain speak to them about what kind of world they were owed and yet never received.

I don't know how the woman whose pregnancy ended in that auto accident was processing her grief a year or three or ten years later. I hope she met a pastor like Kal, willing to sit with her in the midst of her pain, to help honor what was taken from her, and maybe even to let her pain speak to her. Continually bypassing our pain—even in the name of the Lord—only delays our resurrection. Aired grief bravely asserts the inherent worth of our dreams and longings. It acknowledges the unique truth and beauty of individual human lives independent of what these lives earn or accomplish for parents, gods, countries, or global economies. Acknowledged pain exorcizes the demons of productivity and scarcity that rule so much of how we live, why we work, and how we love others and ourselves. This is because our pain and grief are inconvenient demands: that we make unbroken eye contact with the beauty of a world, a life, or a moment that has been lost and will never be recovered. Grief won't ever be popular, marketable, or productive. And that, my friends, is precisely why it is so damn important for us to listen to it. Grief is a guttural expression of faith in a world beyond the one we're living in now. It is the only sermon I'm still willing to sit still for.

Writing after the death of his own teenage son, Bruce Rogers-Vaughn passionately advocates for the "recovery" of grief as that which gives birth to faith:

> But if we have ears to hear, we discover that the cries of grief are
> at the same time the birth pangs of faith. And this is the other

side of the dialectic of faith as it emerges from grief. Grief, if we allow it to appropriately devastate us, breaks the hold that the mesmerizing everydayness of our world has upon our souls. It makes us aware of that deeper reality from which we live and move and have our being. It is only in this sense, it seems to me, that we can speak of God as being present to us. It is a presence that, as in grief, comes not instead of or in spite of absence, but through and by means of absence.

Only when we allow our pain to "appropriately devastate us," as Rogers-Vaughn puts it, can the "mesmerizing everydayness" of what we've come to call normal life be called into question. When we begin naming our pain and loss and grief together, in the presence of one another, it increases the complexity of life and forces us to slow down in a world demanding greater efficiency and increased speed. When humans are allowed to be themselves, they are *complicated*—just like the *Diagnostic and Statistical Manual* taught me to call grief that has lasted for longer than six months. When God is allowed to be truly God, God is complicated. When life is allowed to be truly life, it's incredibly complicated.

Often, in the aftermath of our depressed withdrawal or anxious anger, cultural messaging communicates to us that the problem isn't our often inhumane working conditions or inauthentic relationships but our "feelings" or "emotions." We're told we should "move on" before this emotional instability soon gets the better of us once again. But when we slow down, we know this is a lie because things are always more complicated than that.

It isn't *just* that we feel angry or cynically withdrawn from one another because of some inherent brokenness. It's that our expressions of anger and withdrawal are efforts to cope with far deeper feelings of hopelessness and worthlessness maintained by a system that has monetized our discontent. You don't have to own a "shopping is my therapy" tote bag to understand how so many of us were taught to rebrand our pain as something productive and consumptive. In this

kind of world, it is so terribly important to give a full hearing to the
deep complexity of our feelings before immediately getting stitched
up, freshly medicated, and right back to shopping online. The bury-
ing or reframing of our pain into something more productive isn't
the point of life, good therapy, or effective psychotropic medication.
You're thinking of anesthesia.

Whenever we find ourselves pushed into either anger or hopelessness, us or them, good or bad, more or nothing, we must begin recognizing this for what it is: an effort to sort us, to uncomplicate our
humanity in order to boil us down into the smallest unit of commercial value for someone else's benefit. Instead, when we allow our pain
to speak, it introduces us to the fullness of a life (and a community
of witnesses) defined by both growth and decline, joy and loss, not to
mention sacredness and profanity existing simultaneously. I'm saying
the complexity isn't a curse; it's a blessing. It doesn't drown us; it helps
us float. It doesn't bury us; it resurrects us into a life where we might
conceive of something new on the other side of nihilistic rage and
despondency.

Here's how Brené Brown describes the transformative role that
seeking to understand and listen to our anger and pain can play:
"Anger is a catalyst. Holding on to it will make us exhausted and
sick. Internalizing anger will take away our joy and spirit; externalizing anger will make us less effective in our attempts to create change
and forge connection. It's an emotion that we need to transform into
something life-giving: courage, love, change, compassion, justice.
Or sometimes anger can mask a far more difficult emotion like grief,
regret, or shame, and we need to use it to dig into what we're really
feeling. Either way, anger is a powerful catalyst but a life-sucking
companion."

To undertake this kind of transformative, complicated growth,
we need guides who help us transform our pain into something like
"courage, love, change, compassion, justice." Jesus is a good example
of how this transformation might happen, and hip-hop is another. For
me, few other things convert righteous indignation, profane anger,

and systemic abandonment into something that is wholly, unconquerably, complexly *alive*. I'm saying both Jesus and hip-hop empty my tomb every time.

"I SPEAK TO GOD IN PUBLIC"

In 1996, as a seventh grader, I was formally introduced to the music of Tupac Shakur. Before this moment, I had pretended to be into hip-hop only as a way of creating enough cultural cachet in my suburban middle school to hide the fact that the number-one track on my Sony Discman at the time was Bruce Hornsby and the Range's 1986 hit "The Way It Is." The reason this introduction to Tupac sticks out to me is that his best-selling track, "Changes," actually sampled Hornsby's "The Way It Is" and, in so doing, unexpectedly brought the disparate parts of my bifurcated musical selfhood into harmonious relief. Upon first listen (in a charter bus on an overnight trip to Colonial Williamsburg), I was embarrassingly brought to tears by Shakur's treatment of Black life in the mid-1990s set to Hornsby's synth, leaving my friend Patrick to lean over and ask, "Dude, are you okay? You've been crying and listening to one song for, like, the last hundred miles." I was and I wasn't, Patrick.

Upon entering high school, despite my saving encounter with the sermons of Rev. Shakur, I was soon convinced that hip-hop wasn't really *for* me—that somehow liking hip-hop, listening to it, or valuing it as both a needed and desperately beautiful cultural critique was ultimately beyond the comprehension of a white kid wearing Banana Republic chinos. If I'm being honest, I didn't really know what to do with hip-hop's militant belief that Blackness in America could be simultaneously powerful *and* painful, playful *and* prophetic, tragic *and* hopeful. As a mostly racist white kid, I found hip-hop to be complicated in ways I wasn't (and sometimes still am not) ready for.

So as I aged, I began deriding hip-hop for its repeated use of F-words and N-words; its glorification of violence, crime, and exploitation; and its naive self-aggrandizement in the face of Black poverty and community degradation. Mostly, my refusal to listen to hip-hop then was rooted in a pervasive fear of inauthenticity or gross appropriation. These days, behind the wheel of my Prius—as my son's car seat pushes my knees into the steering wheel—with the factory bass turned to "eleven," I still sometimes worry that I am not only an appropriator of a cultural vocabulary and pain that isn't my own but one who benefits from said culture's repeated degradation.

Amid my own tension in attempting to enjoy hip-hop as a tone-deaf white dude, my good friend Mikey played me Chance the Rapper's 2016 masterpiece, *Coloring Book*. And just like that, I was a tearful seventh grader on the way to Williamsburg all over again. It wasn't just *Coloring Book*'s expressly prophetic, hopeful, and Christian stance toward exploitation and Black liberation that brought me to tears. It was the complexity of it all. With profanity, good humor, gospel choirs, and a track titled "How Great" featuring the rapper Jay Electronica and the contemporary Christian chorus "How Great Is Our God" by Chris Tomlin, Chance reminds us throughout his album that we are always surrounded by both pain and blessing, joy and sorrow, sacredness and profanity—which must be why he finds himself speaking to God "in public," almost constantly.

"I think what [Black liberation theology] has shown us and teaches is that we're very far from an equitable or equal society," Chance told the *New Yorker*, "and that we will be the generation that fixes it . . . I think I am an activist at this point. I think that we should all be activists. I think that we should all be active in the dismantling of white supremacy and then creating a real heaven on earth."

Even if we might be uncomfortable with the verbiage, hip-hop refuses to let us escape from the violent and self-interested philosophy undergirding most of our decision-making here in America. Perhaps the profanely bald-faced honesty, the unrelenting aliveness of it all, is why even deeply racist white teenagers love hip-hop. Hip-hop bravely and unselfconsciously names their grief and their pain.

Cornel West calls this kind of emotional complexity the practice of "tragicomic hope" in the face of hopelessness. The word *tragicomic* might sound a bit off-putting at first, but when we give it enough space to breathe, it offers a kind of complexity that we need—like when you laugh unexpectedly after a good cry because snot is running down the front of your shirt. *That's* tragicomic. For Dr. West, this kind of complicated hope is often found in Black blues and jazz communities, where "righteous indignation" is fully expressed "with a smile and deep inner pain without bitterness or revenge." The enduring relevance and, according to West, emotional maturity of jazz and hip-hop artists are centered not just in the richness of their music but in the ways that their pain has been creatively exorcized and made a servant to hope and love. "When we look down through the corridors of time," he writes, "the black American interpretation of tragicomic hope in the face of dehumanizing hate and oppression will be seen as the only kind of hope that has any kind of maturity in a world of overwhelming barbarity."

Today, pastors, prophets, artists, activists, therapists, teachers, and whole communities formed by suffering are uniquely positioned to introduce us to a mature kind of hope formed by more than just next quarter's earning report or the opportunity to one day own a home with more bedrooms than people in our families. The hope we need now can be found only in the unbreakable self-respect, prophetic joy, and radical okayness of communities that refuse to be defeated by American self-interest, no matter how hard our self-interest presses upon them. This kind of stiff-backed hope tells the truth about how it's actually feeling (sometimes with profanity!) and about what it's like to try to raise kids as a single mom, teach students trapped at home in a global pandemic, attend a crumbling high school, see the doctor in-between shifts at a job that doesn't provide benefits, or be a woman in a STEM career or a person of color in a private equity firm.

In my case—as a tone-deaf white guy wearing an Oxford button-down, bobbing my head along with the rhythmic complexity pouring out of my factory speakers—tragicomic complexity isn't terrifying, overwhelming, or fake. It's liberating. Because it reminds me that even if I'm not self-sufficient, or in control, or put-together, or perfect, like my American folk religion once taught me I had to be, I'm not alone, and neither are you. We never have been. If we let ourselves receive its witness, shared pain and grief have a way of pulling strangers together. I've seen it, I've felt it, I've hugged it. In *The Fire Next Time*, Baldwin calls this kind of moment "integration." He describes it as an act performed "with love" by Black people who subversively force white America "to see themselves as they are" and to prevent us any longer from "fleeing from reality" so that we might, all of us, "beg[i]n to change it." In a world buckling under the weight of unyielding awesomeness, only the voices and witness of the oppressed can save us.

Upon bravely allowing our own and others' pain to speak, we may discover that instead of angrily or hopelessly dying alone, we rise together. Becoming radically okay with airing the pain we've been hiding from one another gives us enough courage to begin confronting the God we grew up with, the prevailing American commitment to self-interest at all costs, and the ways this commitment turns our neighbors into competitors. When we stop internalizing the pain of a hyperventilating economic system long enough to rest and empathize with our grief, we are engaging in an act of political, theological, and interpersonal resistance. Naming our pain out loud in the presence of one another gives us enough stability to properly face and respond to the loss of what each of us was ultimately owed but never actually received—from life, from our own families, from our communities, and most especially, from God.

I'm saying you were owed something more life-giving than a morality and self-worth rooted in how much you earn and where you went to school. Because more awesomeness or productivity won't ever stabilize you; only *enough* can do that. But to talk about that, with both feet planted firmly on the ground, I need to talk about what it was like growing up with my (and possibly your) heavenly Father.

Rather than one more tired sermon about *his* glory, it's time we talked about what living with this heavenly Father was actually like, what it did to us, and what this heavenly Father owes us. I believe that when we, like the disciple Thomas, actually let our doubts about the treatment we've often received at the hands of this God speak for themselves, our depression and anxiety and burnout will bring us face-to-face with something beyond eternal and economic judgment: a new kind of God, a new kind of world, and a new kind of life. Even if the doors are still locked in the face of our fear, the crucified and resurrected heavenly parent you always deserved shows up anyway. We just have to know where to look.

What If We Weren't Afraid of God?

How to Reparent Ourselves

The Christian Scriptures contain stories of a violent warrior God, and of a savior who summons followers to care for the "least of these." The Bible ends in a bloody battle, but it also entreats believers to act with love and peace, kindness, gentleness, and self-control. Contemporary white evangelicalism in America, then, is not the inevitable outworking of "biblical literalism," nor is it the only possible interpretation of the historic Christian faith; the history of American Christianity itself is filled with voices of resistance and signs of paths not taken.

—Kristin Kobes Du Mez, *Jesus and John Wayne*

Several years ago, as I was getting my start as a therapist, I worked as an intern in the counseling center of a tiny liberal arts college. There I treated mostly first-generation college students struggling with anxiety, depression, suicidal ideation, sexual identity, and substance abuse. During my time there, I routinely hid or buried my identity as a former Baptist pastor. I did so out of a supposed respect for student after student who expressed, in answer to my questions about their family history, an abusive, destructive, or toxic connection to Christianity in the distinctly Baptist style.

In her book *Jesus and John Wayne*, historian Kristin Kobes Du Mez succinctly characterizes much of what I was hearing from the students shuffling in and out of my office on campus. Du Mez describes the theology undergirding white evangelicalism (of which Baptists remain a powerful constituent) as one that continues to be ruled by images of Jesus as "a Warrior Leader, an Ultimate Fighter, a knight in shining armor, a William Wallace, a General Patton, a never-say-die kind of guy, a rural laborer with calluses on his hands and muscles on his frame, the sort you'd find hanging out at the NRA convention. Jesus was a badass." This may sound awesome if you're a concealed-carry permit pretending to be a person but less helpful if you tick literally any other demographic survey box. Badass Jesus indiscriminately and violently protects "the faith" from being undermined by the rising forces of secularity and sinfulness—despite the fact that sometimes those "secularizing forces" are our own children and their identities, questions, and safety.

I soon found that Badass Jesus—true to Du Mez's account—left many of the students I was seeing for therapy in precarious situations often involving harrowing accounts of abuse, neglect, and heaping doses of shame in their houses of worship. "Caught up in authoritarian settings where a premium is placed on obeying men, women and children find themselves in situations ripe for power and abuse," writes Du Mez. "Yet victims are often held culpable for acts perpetrated against them; in many cases, female victims, even young girls, are accused of 'seducing' their abusers or inviting abuse by failing to exhibit proper femininity."

Put baldly, Badass Jesus is an embodiment of our self-interested American folk religion. He is a God who, rather than freeing us with his unending strength, continually places responsibility for managing the rather wide scars he leaves behind in the hands of those he abuses, abandons, and consigns to hell. Unlike Rambo, Badass Jesus never comes through for anyone other than himself.

When I was a young college student myself—attempting to carve out a properly holy existence amid the ensnaring influences of what my campus ministers referred to as "the temptations of the flesh"—I attended a men's retreat unironically called "Manmaker." There we watched movies like *Gladiator* and *Braveheart*, whittled "spears" out of wood foraged from the nearby forest, heard our married male ministers regale us with the glories of "hot sex" within the bounds of marriage, and eventually were led up a hiking trail during a snowstorm to throw daggers at a wooden caricature of Goliath. I think at least one of us was shirtless at all times.

It was also during this retreat that we freshly made men were encouraged to write letters to our female friends. These letters were meant to serve as clear guidelines for how these women might encourage "our walk" in pursuit of holy living. One such letter we heard read aloud at the retreat encouraged our "sisters in Christ" to avoid wearing shirts with words on them because this would inevitably force the letter's author to stare at their chests and ultimately imagine them naked. According to this letter, as well as the frequent sermons apprising us of the dangers of masturbation, pornography, and "going too far," the responsibility for holy living seemingly always rested in "the weaker sex." For being so powerful, like Samson before him, Badass Jesus seemed just one deep V-neck away from throwing everything out the window for a moment of hedonic passion.

Back in the college counseling office, my eagerness to abandon my own struggles with the toxically masculine and destructively entitled God I had grown up with often entailed avoiding or gently redirecting God-talk from my psychotherapy patients back to "the real reason" they had begun seeing me in the first place—you know, like depression or something. Luckily, thanks to my own therapist and the gentle prodding of my supervisor, I finally began disclosing to the students in my office that yes, their thirty-one-year-old, unpaid intern therapist was actually (*dramatic pause*) an ordained Baptist minister.

This professional disclosure once led to the following exchange:

Student: "No shit! Can we talk about God in here?"
Me: "Uh, yes, if you think that would be helpful."
Student: "I'd love to. I think about God all the time."

For a pastor who had spent the majority of his adult life preparing to talk to people about God, I was rather shocked by how quickly
word spread on campus that you could speak with a Baptist minister about how your heavenly Father never loved you. It soon seemed,
in the campus counseling office at least, that the "theology" shaping
most of my patients' understandings of God had far more to do with
childhood trauma, depression, and anxiety than with their views on
biblical inerrancy or worship music preferences. Toxic God-talk isn't
just about theology and politics; it's about childhood attachment and
identity formation.

CAN I HAVE A WORD WITH YOUR HEAVENLY FATHER?

As a young person from the South, I was taught never to discuss politics
and religion in mixed company. Those discussions, it often seems, are
typically saved for strangers we shout at through bullhorns in crowded
intersections. This could explain why most of our spiritual conversations here in America are terribly fraught, especially at Thanksgiving.
Writing for the *New York Times* in 2018, author Jonathan Merritt
argues that "god talk" has experienced a steep decline recently, to the
point that "a paltry 7 percent of Americans say they talk about spiritual
matters regularly." Merritt goes further in his treatment of religious
speech, noting the motivations behind an ever-increasing portion of
our country's collective silence on the movements of the divine:

Many people now avoid religious and spiritual language
because they don't like the way it has been used, misused and
abused by others. But when people stop speaking God because

they don't like what these words have come to mean and the way they've been used, those who are causing the problem get to hog the microphone. That toothy televangelist keeps using spiritual language to call for donations to buy a second jet. The politician keeps using spiritual language to push unjust legislation. The street preacher keeps using spiritual language to peddle the fear of a fiery hell. They can dominate the conversation because we've stopped speaking God. In our effort to avoid contributing to the problem, we can actually worsen it.

Like so many other components of modern American life, words like *God*—and *kindergarten, youth sports,* and *self-care*—have been so thoroughly hollowed out and infused with a deep sense of not-okayness that it can be difficult to determine where all the capitalism ends and the religion begins. Across family histories, demographics, and denominations, I regularly encounter an internalized American folk religion ruled over by a heavenly Father who is equally as demanding as our insatiable Market God. Willie James Jennings rightly labeled this God as "white" and "masculinely self-sufficient," with his fits of blistering anger, capricious demands, or a distant aloofness to the problems of his children. It is a God I grew up with—and one whose incarnate form has, for many of my white evangelical brothers and sisters, come to mirror that of our former president, Donald J. Trump. Once again, Du Mez draws out the clear link between white American evangelicalism's toxically masculine God-talk and Trump's ascendancy among the family-values faithful:

Evangelicals hadn't betrayed their values. Donald Trump was the culmination of their half-century-long pursuit of a militant Christian masculinity. He was the reincarnation of John Wayne, sitting tall in the saddle, a man who wasn't afraid to resort to violence to bring order, who protected those deemed worthy of protection, who wouldn't let political correctness get in the way of saying what had to be said or the norms of democratic society keep him from doing what needed to be done. Unencumbered by traditional Christian virtue, he was a warrior in the tradition (if not the actual physical form) of Mel Gibson's William Wallace. He was a hero for God-and-country Christians in the line of Barry Goldwater, Ronald Reagan, and Oliver North, one suited for Duck Dynasty Americans and American Christians. He was the latest and greatest high priest of the evangelical cult of masculinity.

It's terribly difficult to speak of God and Christianity in a world where our "Christian" president brags about sexual abuse and uses riot police to disperse protestors before a photo op where he holds an upside-down Bible in front of a church. *But we must anyway.* During conversations with psychotherapy patients, friends on the internet, and even my own family, there arose a sudden confusion about what the words *Christian, God,* or *truth* actually meant. This is because most of us were white and (for the most part) formerly or currently evangelical.

Now, before firing up the "see, I told you so" machine, I want to be clear here: progressive Christians are just as beholden to internalized capitalism as white evangelicals. If you don't believe me, just try to become an elder as a poor person of color at a downtown Presbyterian church. Whether your God watches MSNBC or Fox News, shops at Whole Foods or Walmart, listens to religious talk radio or NPR, you can always tell the Market God by his fruit. His fruit is bitter. It will only remind us that ultimately, we don't measure up, aren't enough, and never will be because something is wrong with us. If we keep working at it, though, things could change, but no promises.

So I stopped speaking of God for a while because estrangement seemed like the safest bet. Maybe you've had to come to similar conclusions about your own relationship with the heavenly (or earthly) parent who raised you. Either way, it's time we met a more complicated God: one capable of allowing us enough space and freedom to be ourselves, no matter the cost. It's time we met a God willing to die for us, even if we would never return the favor—not because we're somehow ungrateful, selfish, or sinful, but because this is the kind of trustworthy love real parents (both heavenly and otherwise) owe their kids.

LOVE, TRUSTWORTHINESS, AND DESTRUCTIVE ENTITLEMENT

In my psychotherapy practice, I draw heavily from a theory originally referred to as contextual family therapy and more recently as restoration therapy. This tradition argues that all humans—regardless of cellular makeup, nationality, or socioeconomic status—are entitled not only to food, shelter, and water but also to love and "trustworthiness" from their parents. Two of restoration therapy's founders, Terry and Sharon Hargrave, put it this way:

> In short, the aim of [restoration therapy] is to restore as much love and trustworthiness to the individual, family, and relationships as possible. . . . Simply stated, love is the relational language where we as humans learn about our uniqueness, worthiness, and belonging. Trustworthiness, on the other hand, is the language of action where we learn about the reliable process of giving, the fairness and justice of balancing what we receive, and the openness and vulnerability that leads us to a sense of safety and security in relationships. Love informs our identity while trustworthiness forms our sense of safety. Together, this identity and safety form the nouns and verbs of our language of existence. But this combination of identity and safety is fragile because it is taught to us by fragile and flawed people in an often unsafe world.

Restoration therapy argues that because children did not choose to enter the world—and were instead brought into it kicking and screaming—they are owed a debt by those of us doing the choosing and the raising. Our entrance to the world, ideally, is only accompanied by a sacrificial gift of love and trustworthiness effectively delivered to us over the course of our childhood *without expectation for repayment*. Kids are given the free gift to be themselves, to explore who they are, and to experience the warmth and predictability of a secure attachment to their parents that exists independently of the shape and course their development takes.

How much more contrary to the transaction-filled free market could an arrangement be? When I once described this theory to a new patient, she followed with a perfect analogy: "If I had been raised that way, my childhood would have been like the world's best trampoline, constantly propelling me upward and catching me when I come down. Instead, my childhood was like being shoved in a pool with ankle weights while everyone who could help just yelled at me for not swimming hard enough."

The inherently sacrificial character this radical approach to parenthood takes can only be maintained by an equally radical faith. When I say "faith," what I mean is that parents experience "repayment" or a "return on investment" for their sacrificial efforts whenever their children choose to keep both love and trustworthiness in circulation by paying them forward to those coming after them. As increasing amounts of love and trustworthiness are then freely and self-disinterestedly delivered to those we raise, it heals the world, both now and for future generations we have yet to meet. This kind of work is resurrecting because it brings last names, holiday celebrations, and sometimes whole family trees back from the dead.

Yet considering that the formative elements of our interpersonal development are communicated to us by complicated people in an unsafe world, all of us are susceptible to what the psychological literature calls "attachment-based injuries." These injuries—whether occurring in early childhood or even later adolescence—can be generally understood as a disruption in the delivery of love and trustworthiness from our parents or guardians. Attachment-based injuries often leave us with the sense that our identity and safety—what the Hargraves term "the nouns and verbs of our language of existing"—are tethered to our usefulness at satisfying the unmet longings and attachment-based injuries of our own parents, who received those injuries from their parents, who received those injuries from *their* parents, and up the family tree it goes. In a broken world, the only things trickling down are the unmet entitlements of previous generations now resting upon our own young shoulders.

Whether treating low-income, at-risk adolescents in a poorly resourced high school or high-income, married couples from well-to-do families in private practice, I find that the genesis of most family and community distress stems from what psychiatrist Ivan Boszormenyi-Nagy refers to as "destructive entitlement." Boszormenyi-Nagy, the architect of contextual family therapy, argues that whenever the intergenerational flow of love and trustworthiness is disrupted, parents, instead of sacrificially giving love and trustworthiness to their children, begin *demanding* these very things from them instead.

Destructive entitlement is why your dad—who was abandoned by his own father—might have yelled at you in the van all the way home from tee-ball practice for not "hustling" instead of reminding you that even when you fail or come up short, you can always try again. This is because he desperately needed you to be good so he could feel good about being your dad. Destructive entitlement is why you may have spent so much of your adolescence worried about how to please your mom—who was raised by a critical and demanding mother herself—instead of learning to love yourself by watching a mom whose love always held you up, even when you slammed the door in her face. Destructive entitlement is also why one of the first phrases out of my son's mouth whenever he falls down, trips, slips, or spills is "I'm okay!" (even if he isn't). He has already learned—thanks to my incessant interrogations following an injury or an unexpectedly loud noise from his bedroom—that I *need* him to be okay, even if he isn't. So he dutifully complies.

In one interview, Boszormenyi-Nagy describes the fundamental shape of destructive entitlement as "a justice issue," one in which "people recognize that the motivation for revenge is actually driven by a deep sense of justice and a deep loyalty to those who loved but injured us." That is, even if we can't always admit it to ourselves, we know the treatment we received as kids was sometimes (or often) questionable, unfair, or even abusive. As we grow up, these injustices we learned to just sort of live with become thoroughly internalized as core truths, like a splinter gradually enfolded by skin. Our own worthlessness, abandonment, or the feeling of never being enough—these core beliefs then form the foundational narratives and coping responses that guide our decision-making, self-worth, parenting, and, ultimately, our identity. When these injuries stem not just from our fathers or mothers but from our image of a heavenly Father who demands fidelity, love, and trust (or else!)—well, you can imagine just what kind of "deep loyalty to those who loved but injured us" Boszormenyi-Nagy is describing.

DESTRUCTIVE ENTITLEMENT ISN'T JUST FOR FAMILIES

When understood collectively, destructive entitlement often leaves children with an outsized sense of responsibility for earning their place in a world where nothing is freely given and everything must be earned. In capitalism, experiences with destructive entitlement leave us the unwitting victims and perpetuators of abusive workplaces, relationships, and religious and educational institutions for the sake of financial security. This repetitious cycle is thanks to the ways that destructive entitlement—or the experience of having our parents, caregivers, and formative institutions demand love and trustworthiness from us rather than giving these things to us freely—destroys our ability to understand who we are and what we are owed independently of what we produce for others.

For parents who have been raised in this kind of system since birth, resentful burnout is a typical result. Destructive entitlement can frequently end up justifying the outsized sacrifices and expenditures of time, energy, and money we now furiously deliver to our own seemingly "ungrateful" children. When you don't get the kind of love and trustworthiness you needed growing up, you take it from your kids, even if it feels like giving.

Anne Helen Petersen defines our contemporary parenting culture as one that often "enforces ideals that are impossible to achieve within our current caregiving scenarios and squares the blame for societal failures on individual parents." This kind of parenting "breeds resentment and despair—particularly for women who placed stock in the idea of an equal partnership," Petersen argues. Contemporary parenting "equates exhaustion with skill, or aptitude, or devotion: The 'best' parents are the ones who give until there's nothing left of themselves. And, worst of all, there's little evidence that it actually makes kids' lives better." No matter how hard we work to hide it with parenting blogs and limits on screen time, the thing about destructive entitlement is that kids can always tell when we as parents need them to be okay, successful, and good at math for our sake rather than theirs.

Burned-out helicopter parenting and internet-based mom shaming aren't simply manifestations of individual parenting failures; rather, they are the incarnations of a system that constantly internalizes and pathologizes the pain of existing within its world. Our irascible Market God demands constant sacrifice, and because we never received what we were owed from our own fruitless efforts at pleasing this God, so do we. Thus we maintain a system where our hopes and dreams are put on layaway for the next generation of parents, who do the very same thing for their children, who do the very same thing for theirs, *ad infinitum.*

Glennon Doyle lays bare this abusively cyclical myth as she thunders against a culture that defines womanhood specifically (and parenting generally) as an unending effort in "selflessness" that leaves women "numb, obedient, quiet and small." She continues, "Selfless women make for an efficient society but not a beautiful, true, or just one. When women lose themselves, the world loses its way." In the kind of parenting culture Petersen and Doyle define, I fully expect phrases like "sacrificial gifts of love and trustworthiness" and parenting with "no expectation for return" to be interpreted as yet more demands for parents to work harder. Instead, instilling love and trustworthiness in our children is an act of creative, tragicomic okayness where we allow them the gift of being complicated kids raised by complicated parents in a complicated world. Perfection doesn't teach our kids how to float; only trustworthy love when they're afraid of sinking does that. Bottomless investment and attention won't stabilize our children; only radical, complicated okayness in the face of their fear does that.

Destructive entitlement is what I frequently heard working its way through crumbling institutional church systems in the version of American Christianity in which I was raised. Across American churches and denominations, there is a trickle-down demand for children, youth, and young folks to save the church, return to the church, tithe to the church, or honor and respect a church that has so frequently overseen their abuse, neglect, and rejection. In the case of the oppressed—whether they be young, minority, immigrant, female, abused, impoverished, or LGBTQ—faithfulness to God and the church is often translated as a command to keep quiet about their pain or else quietly leave. All of us, no matter what we have experienced at the hands of the faithful, are seen as owing it to God and the church to protect "its witness." When your heavenly Father is Badass Jesus, faith is a lot like signing a nondisclosure agreement for an undisclosed amount of money at the end of things. *Or else.*

If we logically follow the thread, destructive entitlement has a genesis, a source, that stands as the original rift—or sin, if you will. As the story so often goes, once upon a time there was a mistake: a massive misstep when the first humans decided to break a rule and hide from the consequences. This mistake resulted in our heavenly Father expelling us from a place of unending love and trustworthiness and into a world defined by enmity and struggle—because, we were told, *he loved us.* In my Christian tradition, I was regularly taught that this original sin was my fault, and yours, and that we were born covered in its stain. We were consigned to a life in which, depending on your theological tradition, we are to work it off, pray it off, worship it off, or mostly ignore it (except at Christmas and Easter, when we visit church with our parents). From the total depravity of the Reformed theological tradition to the personal responsibility and bootstrapping philosophies of evangelicalism, there is a universality to our desperate efforts at pleasing, posturing, and performing for a distant and mostly disappointed heavenly Dad.

Christianity, in its most disastrous form, preaches a dutiful internalization of cosmic, original, destructively entitled pain because it mandates that "sinners" take responsibility for the disappointment our God must feel whenever he looks upon us wretches. This line of thinking sounds not terribly different from that of middle schoolers who sit in my office and, with tears in their eyes, guiltily admit that they were responsible for the dissolution of their parents' marriage. "Oh," I usually respond. "Well, that makes sense. After all, you *are* twelve years old—and you really stopped making much of an effort when your little brother was born." After this, I quietly smile and sometimes have to wait a beat before they do too.

Then I lean in a little closer and whisper, "You know, there's a term for what you're experiencing. It's called 'parentification.' But you may have heard it pronounced 'bullshit.' It mostly means the same thing."

DIVINE PARENTIFICATION

Like most psychotherapeutic terminology, *parentification* is a made-up word to describe human experiences so familiar that, when you hear them defined, you ask, "I'm paying exactly *how* much an hour for you to tell me something I already know?" Parentification is what happens when a child is implicitly or explicitly mandated by a family system to become a caregiver to his or her parents rather than being reliably cared for by them. While parentification takes many forms, it often involves children performing developmentally inappropriate tasks whenever their parents are incapacitated by addiction, divorce, unemployment, or even their own attachment-based injuries. Parentification happens when children are made to be emotionally stable to avoid "upsetting" their mothers or when children work two jobs to cover the cost of their dads stealing money from their piggybanks to buy weed. It is the internalized responsibility children feel to maintain and even "save" the family system despite the ludicrousness of this messaging whenever we hear them say it out loud.

And now you're likely remembering that kid from high school who fell asleep in English because he worked the night shift to help pay rent—or maybe that was you. One thing you might not know, however, is that one of the most psychologically damaging aspects of parentification is that it often goes unacknowledged. Over a long enough time, it ends up creating an implicit "bind," which "traps" parentified children in a "prolonged compliance with unilateral demands for parentification" as Boszormenyi-Nagy puts it, without the ability to directly comment upon the inappropriateness of their relationships with their caregivers. Arguably, what Boszormenyi-Nagy is saying is that the worst part of parentification isn't that it happens; it is that, over time, we start believing it's normal.

"Dad, what's a deductible," my six-year-old son once asked me, "and why does it have so many zeroes?" Explaining the American health care system to children reminds me of just how right Boszormenyi-Nagy was. These unacknowledged parentified relationships he's describing in his work as a therapist and psychiatrist not only characterize the brokenness within individual family systems wrecked by destructive entitlement; they also illuminate the feeling all of us face whenever we have been functionally abandoned to fend for ourselves by political, ecclesial, and institutional leaders. If you don't know what I mean, may I remind you of what it was like to find reliable public health information in America during a global pandemic.

Parentification is the only way I know to describe living through the nearly endless coronavirus pandemic in the United States. If we were sick, it was up to us to navigate a complicated, underfunded, and byzantine system where a test for the virus could cost anywhere from a few dollars to a few hundred depending solely on where we lived and who was administering the test. If we were well (and lucky), it was almost entirely up to us to decide whether we should send our children to school or keep them at home, host family members outside in masks or eat together normally, all undertaken without clarity or direction from the officials charged with caring for our public health and well-being.

In Tennessee, our pandemic response mirrored the gridlocked nature of our politics, with our conservative county mayor publicly flouting mask mandates, angrily questioning the response of our local Covid-19 task force (of which he was a member), and regularly quarreling with our city's more progressive mayor and her efforts to enforce proactive public health measures. This left the rest of us to, essentially, spend a year turning up the volume on Netflix loud enough to drown out the adults fighting downstairs in the kitchen.

Parentification is also the only way I know how to describe coming of age within a framework of belief mandating the maintenance of my perpetual uneasiness in the presence of a Being who brought me into the world only to become immediately disappointed with my sinfulness at birth. It was my responsibility to glorify God, to praise God, to serve God, and to bear witness to God. If this sacrifice burned me out, swallowed me up, or left my chest anxiously heaving in the middle of the night—well, that was my problem because God is perfect, and, as I was so often reminded by praise and worship choruses, *I am not.*

From the women wearing turtlenecks to avoid being objectified by the men of my undergraduate campus ministry to the girls made to "forgive" their abusers before God and the male pastor who serves as his representative to those of us left emotionally and physically stooped by the pressure of God's "perfect plan" for our lives, our redblooded, badass American Market God has parentified his many children here on Earth. As Rob Bell reminds us, "We shape our God and our God shapes us." So it's time we started acknowledging both what we believe about this God *and* what we believe this God believes about us—as well as what this cycle of belief does to us over time. Otherwise, whether in our belief or unbelief, like Isaac carrying the wood up Mt. Moriah in service to his father Abraham, we end up accidentally participating in our own sacrifice—over and over again.

I say this because there are alternatives to this kind of God and to this kind of faith. In contrast to the white God of toxically masculine self-sufficiency and ownership I grew up with, Black womanist theologian Delores S. Williams roots her God-talk in an image of God most powerfully expressed in the desperate efforts of Abraham's rejected concubine, Hagar, and her cast-off son, Ishmael. Williams argues that for Black women living in racist and patriarchal systems, there is no better image of what the unconquerable love of God looks like than a single mother out of options: "Hagar's situation is congruent with many African-American women's predicament of poverty, sexual and economic exploitation, surrogacy, domestic violence, homelessness, rape, motherhood, single parenting, ethnicity, and meetings with God. Many Black women have testified that 'God helped them make a way out of no way.' They believe God is involved not only in their survival struggle, but that God also supports their struggle for quality of life." When we begin believing in a God who sees us even when we are at the edge of ourselves—a God who knows us truly and is intimately connected to our survival even if it kills her in the process—it changes how we read not just one story in the Bible but all of them. Just ask my son.

DAD, I WANT IT TO BE TRUE

Parenting is your regular reminder that life is mostly a closed loop. A few years ago, as my then four-year-old son and I rocked together in his room before bed, I read him a story from an updated version of the very same *Illustrated Children's Bible* I, as a child worried about my own postmortem future, had furiously thumbed through years earlier. After a brief read of Jesus's miraculous water-walking in Matthew 14, my son asked me an important question: "Dad, is this story true?"

Almost immediately, I was drawn into images and memories of conversations I had been privy to over the years about biblical inerrancy, infallibility, orthodoxy, and heresy, as well as all the moments my questions and doubts and fears were met with a reminder to answer things the right way . . . *or else.* I started to sweat and began stammering some sort of answer involving the ways that ancient Near Eastern hagiography would sometimes embellish parts of an important person's life story to make them more memorable for later listeners. This was, obviously, a nonstarter for my boy. But in a moment of accidental parental genius (or the interruption of what TV preachers call the *Holy Ghost!*), I stopped talking and asked my son, "I don't know, man, what do you think?"

Without blinking, he looked up at me and said, "Dad, I want it to be true."

And right there, in the middle of a bedtime routine we had done together for years, I found myself wiping my eyes in the presence and possibility of a God that I actually *wanted* to believe in and not one I was forced to worship . . . or else. For much of my life, I had been warned that trusting my own dreams of what God could be like was a thoroughly sinful endeavor: *"All other ground is sinking sand, Eric."* But in the mouth of my son, this longing for a God worth believing in seemed foundational, organic, and full of endless possibilities. I found myself wanting to believe in this God and wanting my son to as well.

When my son proclaims that he *wants* the story of Jesus to be true, he is saying that the story compels him—not because he needs it to be true in order to go to heaven after he dies, because it changes how I look at him when he answers the wrong way, or because he has already internalized his parentified role as someone propping up God's ever-tenuous hold on "glory." When he says he wants it to be true, the ground breaks open, stones roll away, tombs empty, and dead things come back to life—for him, but mostly for me.

In restoration therapy, our approach to treatment sometimes involves a therapist leading a patient through an experiential exercise where he or she is invited to imaginatively return to childhood, reencounter pain from a particular moment in that past, and interrupt it by providing the kind of love and trustworthiness he or she was always owed but never received. This is called "reparenting," and it is typically confined to the therapy office. True to its name, reparenting is an act of creatively becoming our own fathers and mothers to speak to, name, and heal what was broken in the past and, ultimately, to change the way we live in the future.

So when my own son looks up at me during bedtime, like I once did to my own father, and asks me what kind of God we're dealing with here, I am given an opportunity to see myself in his eyes and in his question. I can answer it the way I was taught, I can ignore it, or I can slow down and do something brand-new. Most of life, I'm finding as I get older, is an invitation for me to become the kind of human I needed much earlier.

What better term than *reparenting* exists for this—the moment when our own child looks up at us and expresses the same fears and asks the same questions we once put to our own parents at bedtime? In that kind of moment, we are brought face-to-face with our past, present, and future all at once. It then requires very little imagination to wonder what it might be like to interrupt the cycles of trickle-down pain, destructive entitlement, and parentification by delivering to someone else the kind of parenting to which *we* were entitled. This is not just because our kids deserve to come of age in a world shaped by this kind of love and trustworthiness but because we do as well.

Instead of spending a lifetime demanding love and trustworthiness from people who don't owe them to us (like our kids!), we finally encounter our longed-for restoration precisely when we recognize that the only way to receive what we were owed, from our own families and our own gods, is to deliver these things to others in the same way we wanted them to be delivered to us. When we experience this kind of salvation or restoration, it won't come thanks to some karmic repayment plan for putting good and selfless things out into the universe. It will come because we will have resurrected our connection to a divine force who desires only to care for and love the world—and who does so totally independently of how that world cares for and loves God in return. Reparenting continually provides us opportunities to re-create the world in the image of the God Hagar meets in the wilderness and the God I met at Trader Joe's. Whenever we come up short, feel burned out, spectacularly fail, or anxiously keep trying to please the Market God, what if we could treat ourselves like we would treat a child we dearly love independently of what they produce, earn, or *do* for us? Jesus famously called this sort of thing loving others as we love ourselves. When I see my son leaning against my chest, hearing for the very first time the story of a God who walks on waves, I can tell him this story the way I always wanted it told to me. When I do it for him, I hear it too. And when I love him the way I always wanted to be loved by my own father, I feel this kind of love too.

What I believe the Son of God is describing in his oft-quoted and sometimes burnout-inducing command to "love your neighbor as yourself" is this miraculous, almost cellular hope that bubbles up inside all of us when we first meet ourselves in the eyes of a child who has just smiled at us for the first time while filling his diaper. Just like there is this miraculous, almost cellular hope that bubbles up inside of us when we first meet ourselves in the eyes of an adolescent who has our selfsame fear of not measuring up to life's impossibly high standards. Just like there is this miraculous, almost cellular hope that bubbles up inside of us when we first meet ourselves in the eyes of a young mom who is exhausted, spit-stained, and desperate for an uninterrupted night of sleep. Even though we're incredibly cynical and our backs hurt far more than they used to, when we love our neighbors in the ways we deserved to be loved as kids, we remake the world in the image of a God who loves without expectation for return. When we love our neighbors in the ways we deserved to be loved as kids, it returns our feet to solid ground. Despite its reference to "ourselves," this love remains resolutely non-self-interested.

Instead of leveraging the lives of the humans in front of us out of an anxious pursuit of our own salvation, we can begin reparenting ourselves and others in the presence of a God who refuses to give up on her kids, no matter what. In a world run by the Market God, reparenting is a labor of resistance, in which we attempt to create a world filled with the kinds of parents, adults, humans, and partners we needed years ago but possibly never received.

If there's anything the self-interested, toxically masculine Trump presidency and the fraying democracy it has wrought have taught us, it's that we have to live in the world we work to create. Unacknowledged destructive entitlement and the parentification that soon follows it have real consequences not just for families but for societies, democracies, and the rising centigrade of the entire planet.

Reparenting provides us powerful, incarnate encounters with a kind of self-*dis*interested love that interrupts the ways our attachment-based injuries drive cycles of self-interested coping, destructive entitlement, and parentification. Reparenting hears our pain, looks us in the eyes, and sets our feet solidly upon a forgotten truth at the center of all this pain—namely, that when you, I, and even the Creator of the Universe simultaneously give what we always needed to people who can never pay us back, we are participating in what my Jewish friends call *tikkun olam*, or the "repair of the world." We repair and re-create the world through tiny acts of restorative justice. Refusing to perpetuate the violence of what was done to us by reparenting the world in front of us isn't just brave, or sacrificial, or martyring. Offering love and trustworthiness is saving *for all of us*, including you—even if it does sometimes feel like a bad investment and even if it seems a bit like dying.

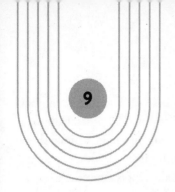

What If We Weren't Afraid of Dying?

How to Do More Than Live Forever

> Can human beings have a disinterested faith in God—
> that is, can they believe in God without looking for
> rewards and fearing punishments? Even more specifi-
> cally: Are human beings capable, in the midst of unjust
> suffering, of continuing to assert their faith in God and
> speak of God without expecting a return?
>
> —Gustavo Gutiérrez, *On Job*

I have never been more mistreated, verbally abused, or threatened with physical harm by fully grown adults than during the summers I called balls and strikes for ten-year-olds playing baseball. As a college student, umping games at the local ball fields where years earlier I had played baseball as an elementary and middle schooler, I had a man tell me he was going to "follow me home" after I struck his son out on a pitch he thought was "way outside." Sadly, this was not even rock bottom for me as a pimply, part-time Little League pariah. Rock bottom was when—following a close call at third base that did not go in favor of my ten-year-old brother's baseball team—my mother loudly accused me of being biased against my own family in front of a bleacher full of people we had known for years. In a ham-handed show of force, I threatened to eject her between innings.

In May 2018, the *Chicago Tribune* cited a report from the twenty-seven thousand–member National Association of Sports Officials that found that "nearly 87 percent of officials experienced verbal abuse, and most believed they were treated unfairly by both coaches and spectators." This consistently poor treatment is combined with the relatively low pay and grueling schedules of youth sports officials, often involving late nights on freezing fields after a full day of work. The result is a "shortage of referees and umpires in youth and high school leagues across the country. The shortage spans all sports and competitive levels, local league representatives say, and has organizers scrambling to staff games."

According to the *Tribune*, the pervasive and worsening mistreatment of officials and referees across all ages and skill levels is due to what psychologist Bruce Svare refers to as "a conflict between what parents want and what their kids want." "Adults want to win; they want scholarships for their kids. Sometimes it's about living out a misspent youth or sports career of their own," Svare argues. "It shouldn't be about them at all. It's about kids and whether or not they are deriving enjoyment in what they're doing."

In terms of contemporary parenting best practices, destructive entitlement may appear culturally orthodox in that it quite often involves the investment of incredible amounts of parental time, money, and effort on behalf of The Kids, who supposedly benefit from all this attention and energy. Yet as discussed much earlier, research shows a growing correlation between the amount of parental time and money spent on youth sports and the *diminishment* of pleasure in those children still playing them.

When we are in our right minds, we have a better than decent chance of recognizing the sheer ludicrousness of threatening to fight the nineteen-year-old psychology major behind home plate. But logic quickly flies out the window in the face of decreasing opportunities for our children in an increasingly unequal society ruled by competition and scarcity. When every moment is lived for "the future," it's almost impossible to pay attention to what's happening to all of us in the present. Self-interested American folk religion mandates that when push comes to shove and sacrifices are required, we parents certainly won't have our Little Leaguer prevented from reaching his full potential by an umpire "with an agenda." This is true even if that umpire lives in our basement and calls us Mom.

HUMAN CAPITAL AND CRUCIFIXION

In a world in which everything is for sale, we humans don't just own capital or spend capital; we become it. Almost constantly, American capitalism funnels the complexity of our values, souls, skills, and identities down to the smallest unit of commercial value. This process takes something transcendent—like your seven-year-old and her growing dandelion collection out in left field—and operationalizes her for consumption by turning her into a product or brand or "future" that we must constantly cultivate and loudly remind to "Hustle!" Anne Helen Petersen, referencing the work of Malcolm Harris, understands human capital as the "future earnings" or "imagined price" of a particular person and his or her work. Functionally, this ideology boils down every moment of our childhood into less of an experience of learning and more of a kind of "preparation for future work."

Peterson and Harris note the ways in which "building value" in our current system results in a transformation of pickup games and hobbies into semipro, year-round soccer teams and twice-weekly violin lessons. Building value is never clearer than in our educational system, where "practicing your times tables or taking a standardized test or writing an essay isn't learning, but *preparing yourself to work.*" This, for Petersen, represents "an incredibly utilitarian view of education, implying that the ultimate goal of the system is to mold us into efficient workers, as opposed to preparing us to think, or be good citizens."

Human capital is an effective way of understanding how capitalism corrupts our educational policies and parenting practices. It also illuminates the ways my childhood evangelical tradition so often discussed the historic Christian doctrine of incarnation: the belief that God fully inhabits the words, teachings, and personhood of Jesus of Nazareth. Growing up, I believed the power and glory of Jesus Christ possessed value for the faithful insofar as it led directly to his crucifixion and, more pointedly, to our future salvation. In the stories, sermons, songs, and children's programming that made up the bulk of my evangelical spiritual formation, a proper presentation of the gospel required a direct recounting of how the sacrificial death of Jesus resulted in the "expiation" or "satisfaction" of God's wrath in the face of human sin. Just like degrees in the humanities and vacation photos that never make it to Instagram, sermons without a direct reference to the death of Jesus and the role this violent death plays in saving humans from hell were believed to be worthless. Depending on your context, they might even be "heretical."

When I said that I have never been more frequently mistreated than when I was an umpire, I may have engaged in hyperbole. This is because I was also a pastor in Southern Baptist churches, youth camps, and professional circles. In these spaces, your credentials were constantly judged according to the degree to which you compellingly delivered the good news of Jesus's saving death on the cross. The complex and contradictory nature of Jesus's actual human life and teachings—not to mention the four somewhat different accounts of this life and these teachings contained in the Gospels in the New Testament and the near-constant Christian confusion over how to properly implement said life and teachings—all find themselves happily washed away by a proper understanding of "the blood of the Lamb." Anytime that questions about the nature of the gospel bubbled up at his church, a millennial pastor friend was fond of saying, "These evangelicals, man, are like vampires: they only want Jesus for his blood."

If it seems altogether unthinkable that mothers and fathers might scream obscenities at referees during their seven-year-olds' soccer game, may I direct your attention to the white-hot rage of evangelicals who have had their pastor openly question the reality of hell, affirm LGBTQ individuals, and condemn white supremacy? Penal substitutionary atonement theory—the belief that God was so angry at human sin that God had to kill Jesus in order to avoid killing everyone else—serves as a kind of theological funnel that drains both complexity and weirdness from Christianity. But I was often told in my days as a Baptist youth pastor that without this grounding principle, Christians remain in constant danger of sliding down a slippery slope toward secular destruction.

Human capital serves a similar organizing function in our society in that it boils civilization, childhood, parenting, education, and religion down into a market-driven struggle for unending growth and future earning potential. In this capitalist tradition (which is also a theological tradition), what is "God" if not an insatiable and thoroughly internalized demand for more? What is "heaven" if not a bottomless bettering and eternal expansion of a life that was formerly subject to what Conor Oberst once called "the shackles of language and measurable time"? When pouring out of the mouths of many white American Christians, terms like *eternal security* and *orthodoxy* are a ravenously spreading cancer that distends any effort at living a life of meaning, authenticity, and true faith. When the good news of Christianity is primarily presented as one more way of surviving the pain of death and human limitation, it reflects a wrongheaded belief that self-interest can ever save anyone and that more—of everything—will one day be fulfilling.

In his book *My Bright Abyss*, which outlines the prospect of a life cut short by a rare and rapidly progressing bone cancer, poet Christian Wiman argues that we "must let go of all conception of what eternity *is*, which means letting go of who *you* are, in order to feel the truth of eternity and its meaning in your life—and in your death." The Market God that sits at the heart of American folk religion cannot help us figure out what words like *gospel* or *good news* or *salvation* or *faith* mean primarily because this God refuses to die, to ever contemplate its own end. An inability to consider the possibility of their own deaths, to let go of who they are, as Wiman might put it, is why most dominant American Christian churches cannot help us define what good news looks like anymore once it has been divorced from the constant accumulation of power, access, and financial solvency. White American Christianity, just like our kids' semipro baseball teams, has been transformed into one more endless effort at grinding, working, earning, or worrying enough about the future that we might one day, finally, be able to predict and ultimately control it.

Despite what I was always promised, *security* or *confidence* aren't the words I'd use to describe my own or others' emotional state underneath this kind of faith tradition. Instead, I might say burned out, exhausted, anxious, and far too terrified to ever stop praising, praying, and proclaiming—because to stop is to doubt, and to doubt is to begin sliding down the slippery slope toward failure, and to fail is to become worthless and valueless and, ultimately, to die forever. This is what all this bottomless effort has always been about anyway, right—not dying? "Sometimes God calls a person to unbelief," Wiman intones, "in order that faith may take new forms."

What if Christianity were interested in teaching us not how to live forever but how to be alive right now in the midst of our pain? And if Christian faith begins and ends with God, what if Christianity, like Thomas once found, is concerned with doubting the water in which we've all been anxiously swimming? At bottom, what if Christianity is less about how much faith we can muster in God and more about a God who inexhaustibly believes in *us*?

For the first Christians, the phrase "dying to self" was a regular way of framing faithfulness in a world ruled by fear, violence, and power. It reflected the radical origins of a faith tradition rooted in the death and resurrection of a man these early Christians believed was God in the flesh. This God's death and resurrection drove them to take risks, to share possessions freely, and to ask questions about everything and everyone around them. This radical, constant questioning is why they called it becoming "born again." Two thousand years later, dying to our self-interest still changes everything about how we live in a world ruled by fear, violence, and power, but only if we believe in a God willing to go first. What if the God you believe in was willing to be doubted, to be replaced—to die, even—so that all of us might be free? And what if letting go of your own self-interested efforts at believing and surviving in the name of this God, instead of drowning you, finally allowed you to float?

NEXT TIME YOU THINK YOU'RE PERFECT, TRY WALKING ON WATER

Here in East Tennessee, while I enjoyably remain within a stone's throw of Cracker Barrel at all times, there *are* trade-offs. The humidity, for one. A crippling reliance on libertarian politics to fund our schools and roads, for another. From time to time, thanks to my ancestral home's deep-seated love of our Lord and Savior Jesus Christ, I also come upon an idling bumper inviting me to reflect upon my next move were the 2015 Honda Odyssey in front of me to suddenly find itself "unmanned" following the soon-coming rapture. Several years ago, one such bumper sticker left me feeling, if not personally attacked, at least confused. It passive-aggressively demanded that I reflect upon my lack of perfection during not one but two gridlocked light cycles: "Next time you think you're perfect, try walking on water."

In the first book of the New Testament, Matthew, we happen upon perhaps one of the most flannelgraphed experiences of Jesus's life, the story where he walks on water, which my son once asked about right before bed. In Matthew 14, we find Jesus, after a long day of teaching and healing, dismissing his disciples to a sleepless night in a boat out on the Sea of Galilee while he goes off by himself to pray and reflect in the surrounding hills. During the middle of the night, the disciples quickly stir to life at the sight of what they believe to be a ghost meandering out to them on the water. But they needn't worry, it's just Jesus, doing something impossibly bizarre in the middle of the night, as usual.

After Jesus smartly identifies himself to the boat of shaken followers, one of his closest disciples, Peter, makes a rather strange request:

"Lord, if it is you, command me to come to you on the water" (Matthew 14:28). And here I'll quote several verses of Matthew 14: "[Jesus] said, 'Come.' So Peter got out of the boat, started walking on the water, and came toward Jesus. But when he noticed the strong wind, he became frightened, and beginning to sink, he cried out, 'Lord, save me!' Jesus immediately reached out his hand and caught him, saying to him, 'You of little faith, why did you doubt?' When they got into the boat, the wind ceased. And those in the boat worshiped him, saying, 'Truly you are the Son of God'" (Matthew 14:29–33).

Most interpretations I've encountered over the years suggest that what suddenly pulls Peter under the choppy Galilean waves is his lack of faith in the divinity and power of Jesus. Like I was taught about the frail faith of doubting Thomas, if only Peter had believed more strongly in the water-walking, wonder-working Son of God, this line of thinking goes, then he would have been able to move mountains and maybe even clip his fingernails too short without them bleeding. But Peter doesn't believe enough, so he almost drowns. (Incidentally, this interpretation seems almost like a word-for-word rendering of the way that millennial patient of mine in chapter 8 conceived of her own childhood: it "was like being shoved in a pool with ankle weights while everyone yelled at me for not swimming harder.")

I can't tell you how many times I regurgitated this exact interpretation of Jesus and Peter's experience together out on the Sea of Galilee for rooms full of earnest young people eager to get God to love them, notice them, or just remember to call them on their birthdays. I read the Bible this way because I was afraid for my own security, both financially and eternally. This fear drove an awful lot of what I ended up saying out loud about things none of us know for sure.

When I stopped getting paid to believe in God, I stopped reading the Bible for a bit. But then later I started reading it again, this time from a place of actual interest and not professional courtesy to those paying for my health insurance. And it's amazing what kind of details suddenly started materializing. This was especially true whenever I began reading the stories of Jesus open-mindedly, from the beginning, and alongside all the other confused characters in the story just trying to make it to work on time. This is a different way of reading Scripture than how I was taught. Growing up, and much later as an employee of Baptist churches and youth camps, I was instructed to read the Bible backward, from the ending—or, I should say, from a triumphant future where all of us already know who wins and what all the right answers are. In this new future, on the other side of people referring to me as "reverend" in mixed company, I started reading the Bible like my son does, which directly impacts how we might understand Peter's doubts.

For instance, if we read Matthew's story forward, from a place of open-handed wonder, we can see that what Peter doubts isn't Jesus or even his miraculous bending of space and matter. Why else would Peter have even bothered to ask Jesus to invite him out on the water in the first place? If Peter didn't believe it was feasible for the Messiah to be standing on the surface of a windy sea, he wouldn't have invited himself along. I would argue that what Peter doubts is whether *he*, Peter, was the kind of fellow who could walk on a normally fluid substance in the middle of the night. Peter doesn't doubt Jesus in the face of high winds and higher waves. Peter doubts Peter. And in so doing, Peter reminds all of us of what it's like to fail in public—before God and everybody, as my grandmother used to say. Mercifully, Jesus reaches out his hand, thus saving Peter from a watery grave, and gently asks him, "You of little faith, why did you doubt?" The possible subtext is "Why did you doubt *yourself*?" and probably not "How dare you doubt *me*?"

This is just one story, and an inarguably cool one at that, but when conceived of in the way I'm describing, Christianity ceases to be a religion dedicated to propping up the fickle ego of a hard-to-please heavenly Father and becomes a religion bringing us face-to-face with a God who stubbornly believes in *us*, no matter how many times we sink. Whenever I read the stories of Jesus through the eyes of my son, I encounter a God continually interested in washing our feet, being replaced by us, dying for us, and somehow still showing up for us even after we've killed him for theological, financial, and political reasons, all without wishing for anything other than peace and stability to be with us. The kind of divine parent we meet throughout the Bible—if we're willing to read with eyes remade for wonder—makes mistakes, gets angry, and sometimes even wishes to quit parenting altogether. But this God is still willing to be doubted, to be raged against, and to be called a moron by an angry teenager at Target. If you don't believe me, just ask Job.

DISINTERESTED RELIGION

In his groundbreaking book *On Job: God Talk and the Suffering of the Innocent*, theologian Gustavo Gutiérrez argues for a thorough reimagining of the true heart of Christian faith. As a Peruvian Catholic priest serving impoverished parishes in the mid- to late-twentieth century, Gutiérrez regularly witnessed how a church structure that prized power and institutional security often maintained the suffering of the poor and oppressed. This led him to wonder,

> How are we to proclaim the God of life to men and women who die prematurely and unjustly? How are we to acknowledge that God offers us a free gift of love and justice when we have before us the suffering of the innocent? What words are we to use in telling those who are not even regarded as persons that they are the daughters and sons of God? . . . The center of the world—so called because the crucified Jesus dwells there, and with him all who suffer unjustly, all the poor and despised of the earth—is the place from which we must proclaim the Lord.

Amid the innocent suffering that characterizes the book of Job, Gutiérrez not only discovers a way to speak more authentically of pain from within his Christian tradition; he allows the experiences of the oppressed to transform the purpose of Christianity from the ground up. Gutiérrez understands this transformation as a process of converting Christianity from a faith dedicated to its own self-interest and eternal security into what he calls a "disinterested" form of religious practice. When Gutiérrez uses the word "disinterested," he isn't describing how you felt as a middle schooler playing tic-tac-toe in the back pew of your childhood church. He's doing something far more radical. Disinterested religion is a kind of faith that asks you to believe in something other than the salvation of yourself, your church, your family, and your way of life. It is a posture expressly rejecting self-interest as the foundation of sound economic, political, and theological belief. In the wake of his transformative encounter with the suffering of the innocent, Gutiérrez compellingly asks, "Can human beings have a disinterested faith in God—that is, can they believe in God without looking for rewards and fearing punishments? Even more specifically: Are human beings capable, in the midst of unjust suffering, of continuing to assert their faith in God and speak of God without expecting a return?" Jesus once said something similarly to his disciples in the face of their questions about the necessity of his own soon-coming death at the hands of the Romans: "For those who want to save their life will lose it, and those who lose their life for my sake will find it" (Matthew 16:25).

Think about this question for a moment and be honest: Would you believe in God if you didn't get anything for believing in God? Would you sign your kid up for travel baseball if it wasn't out of some sort of nascent hope that he would earn a scholarship? Would you have pushed your daughter into chess if it didn't look good on her resume? Would you continue to read, sing, pray, and dutifully attend church if none of it had anything to do with what happens after you die? Essentially, what if the belief itself—or the act of believing amid so many other competing claims for our devotion and attention—was never a means to salvation in the future but an experience with salvation itself, right now? Gutiérrez argues that this question—about the possibility of a faith that exists independent of self-interest—is at the heart of the biblical book of Job.

DOES JOB FEAR GOD FOR NOTHING?

In his commentary creatively entitled *Job*, Samuel Balentine introduces the complexity and power of Job as representing "the crown jewel of biblical literature." Balentine stakes this claim on Job's premise that one can actually speak "rightly" of the divine—as God attests of Job in the whirlwind conclusion of the book—especially when one speaks authentically in the midst of crippling pain and devastation. "From the philosophical ruminations of David Hume (1711–76), to the dramatization of the Joban story in *J.B.* (1956) by the playwright Archibald MacLeish," Balentine writes, "to the ruminations of Rabbi Harold Kushner in *When Bad Things Happen to Good People* (1981), the question that dogs human existence remains essentially unchanged: If God is just and good, why do the innocent suffer and the guilty thrive?"

In the beginning of Job, we encounter a rather strange exchange in the heavenly realm between what the text refers to as "the Satan" and God. In their unfolding conversation, the Satan poses a question that ends up framing the next forty or so chapters of the book: "Does Job fear God for nothing? Have you not put a fence around him and his house and all that he has, on every side? You have blessed the work of his hands, and his possessions have increased in the land. But stretch out your hand now, and touch all that he has, and he will curse you to your face" (Job 1:9–11). Essentially, the Satan is asking God whether Job actually believes in God or just in God's ability to reward him—as the text makes clear in its earlier description of Job's marked fertility, wealth, and faithfulness.

Despite his rather dicey public image, the Satan kind of has a point here. Wouldn't it be stupid *not* to believe in God if worldly and eternal success were tethered to the maintenance of your ongoing belief? God accepts the Satan's premise and then proceeds to stand by as the Satan lays waste to Job's life. By the second chapter, we find a humbled Job atop the ashes of his former life, scratching himself with broken pottery shards and mumbling to the skies. An important reminder: *these are just the first two chapters of a forty-two-chapter book.*

The story really hits its stride when Job's three friends—Eliphaz the Temanite, Bildad the Shuhite, and Zophar the Naamathite—enter stage right and proceed (after sitting shiva silently with Job for a week) to provide theological commentary on the dire straits befalling their friend. Eliphaz notes the seemingly straightforward logic that God doesn't just inflict this kind of damage without a good reason: *so, Job, you must have done something to deserve this*. Bildad argues that God is always wise and benevolent—far wiser and more benevolent than us mere mortals, mind you—and that God's ways are mysterious: *so don't ask questions, Job, unless you want more of the same suffering*. Zophar brings it home with a word reminding us that God is in the process of teaching his people what is good, just, and right in every situation: *so, Job, you have something to learn. Repent and pay attention*.

Our theological responses to catastrophe haven't changed all that much over the years, have they? Which begs one more question: For whom, exactly, are most of these responses to suffering given? Before answering, take a glance at Job's response to his friends in chapter 13:

> Look, my eye has seen all this, my ear has heard and under-stood it. What you know, I also know; I am not inferior to you. But I would speak to the Almighty, and I desire to argue my case with God. As for you, you whitewash with lies; all of you are worthless physicians. If you would only keep silent, that would be your wisdom! . . . Will you speak falsely for God, and speak deceitfully for him? Will you show partiality toward him, will you plead the case for God? Will it be well with you when he searches you out? Or can you deceive him, as one per-son deceives another? . . . Your maxims are proverbs of ashes, your defenses are defenses of clay. (Job 13:1–5, 7–9, 12)

Scholars who have spent years mining the pages of Job refer to this particular chapter as a "courtroom drama," in which Job is judge and jury in a case against the divine. In keeping with the theme, Eliphaz, Bildad, and Zophar are God's character witnesses, providing testi-mony on God's behalf. With this imagery firmly in place, Job's words take on an even darker tone: "You whitewash with lies. . . . Will you speak falsely for God? . . . Will you show partiality toward him?" And my personal favorite: "Your defenses are defenses of clay" (Job 13:4, 7, 8, 12). The heart of Job's complaint is that his friends seem incapable of understanding his pain as anything but an impediment to their own security. The theologizing and pathologizing of Job's pain as an individual failure of morality or belief is little more than thinly veiled self-interest pretending to be orthodoxy—which seems rather familiar.

A GOD WHO LOVES FREELY AND GRATUITOUSLY

Hang around Christians long enough and you will eventually be encouraged to consider the infallibility of God's plan, God's perfection, or God's timing when your life suddenly finds itself unraveling. If you are or ever have been in Christian circles, I want you to pause and think back to when your own pain, loss, marriage, joy, or unpopular confusion was suddenly bypassed in favor of God's ongoing brand maintenance. Imagine this spiritual bypassing as the opposite of that standard breakup line: It's not God; it's *you*.

To be fair, I'm giving Christians a hard time, especially the variety that I grew up around. Religiously maintained self-interest of all varieties does this sort of silencing and bypassing all the time. What if the issue for those of us defending God in the midst of human tragedy isn't that we feel bad for others but rather that we feel bad for *us*? I'm saying that most of our God-talk amid the crises of other people has everything to do with what *we* believe, fear, worry about, and need to be true when life seems out of control rather than what the suffering actually need from us. Speaking personally, when a kid from a divorced family feels alone all the time, what he needs isn't a sermonette about the end of the world or his unending sinfulness. He needs a God who hears his pain and believes him.

What if almost all of our well-reasoned and theologically accurate religious practice is just a more orthodox way of using God as but one more painkiller or existential distraction from a world ruled by scarcity, fear, and chaos? Slippery slope, indeed.

To my mind, the most revelatory scene with Job's friends and all their God-talk occurs when he accuses them of lying *on behalf* of God. Rather than swallowing, praying, or explaining away his pain, Job allows it enough room to speak truthfully about what often passes for theological orthodoxy or right belief. Most of this kind of God-talk represents, at root, a narcissistic effort on the part of the faithful to protect, defend, or stand up for God in order to secure a greater share in God's unfolding economy *no matter the cost*. "I think they're just trying to save their own asses" is probably what a world-weary-Job would have said had your Bible study leader allowed that sort of talk on a Sunday morning. I love Job for the same reason I love hip-hop: he tells the truth even when it requires profanity.

Job's accusation cuts straight to the heart of what has become of much of what passes for faithful Christian practice within American capitalism. When Christians believe that financial success and access to power are the surest metrics of our holiness, that eternity has a cut list, and that our God is a notoriously disappointed and destructively entitled heavenly Father, it is impossible to see the suffering of others as anything else but a relief and a warning. How else could the separation of migrant children from their parents at our country's southern border have been seen and even championed as a justifiable immigration policy by an overwhelming majority of white evangelical Christians? How else could this same community lend ongoing support to the death penalty despite their own God's innocent execution at the hands of the global superpower occupying his homeland?

If we allow it to speak, however, the book of Job comes to quite different conclusions on what it means to talk "rightly" of the divine. As Gutiérrez argues, "It is important that we be clear from the outset that the theme of the Book of Job is not precisely suffering—that impenetrable human mystery—but rather how to speak of God in the midst of suffering. The question that concerns the author is the possibility of disinterested religion, of believing 'for nothing;' in his view only a faith and behavior of this kind can be offered to a God who loves freely and gratuitously."

Whenever we slide, exhausted, to the bottom of life, the God we meet there refuses to be standardized, owned, controlled, hashtagged, branded, or protected. God is the slippery slope, and God is the bottom. As the conclusion of Job attests, the God we meet makes sea monsters, controls the winds, and sets the stars in the firmament. This God is complicated, mysterious, enigmatic, and confusing, but in the best sense of these words.

After God has been harangued, put on trial, and violently disparaged by the lead character for the better part of thirty chapters, God finally addresses the problem, Job's friends: "My wrath is kindled against you and against your two friends; for you have not spoken of me what is right, as my servant Job has" (Job 42:7). Rather than pushing us up a slope of endless perfectionism, performance anxiety, and pain, God is instead patiently waiting on us to sink to the bottom of whatever we've been desperately trying to climb.

Like all good parents, God refuses to be uprooted, destabilized, or embarrassed in the presence of our pain. Job's doubt, just like that of Thomas and Peter, doesn't anger God or keep God away, as I was so often warned as a child. Instead, doubt seems to awaken the kind of God we always wanted to believe in but were told not to. The God Job meets is one who sits on the edge of the bed when we've just cussed her out in front of company, pulls us in close, and whispers to us that life is complicated, and confusing, and complex but that it's also unexpectedly beautiful. God then reminds us that we aren't alone, even when we sink or swear or spectacularly fail.

If we read this story forward rather than backward, we find that instead of sacrificing us—or expecting us to sacrifice others in her name—this God even willingly fails, loses, and dies so that her kids might finally be set free.

IF THERE WAS NO HELL, WOULD
YOU STILL BE A CHRISTIAN?

I once had a friend who taught an Introduction to the New Testament course for first-year students at a conservative Christian university. He took it upon himself to begin every class of each new semester with one simple question: "If there was no hell, would you still be a Christian?"

At this institution, his question was both notorious and deeply subversive. Faculty at the school often found themselves threatened with termination when they expressed ideas that diverged from the accepted beliefs of the denomination that financially kept the school afloat. Despite this oxygen-deprived theological climate, my friend persisted in posing his question to new crops of undergraduates each semester. He eventually resigned—not because he was terribly edgy, but because he remained interested in finding out what actually motivates any of us to believe in God.

In 2012, Kelefa Sanneh profiled former evangelical megachurch pastor Rob Bell for the *New Yorker*. The profile appeared just after Bell had stepped down from his role as the lead teaching pastor of Mars Hill Bible Church in Grand Rapids following the publication of his controversial and *New York Times* best-selling book about hell, *Love Wins*. In the piece, Sanneh outlines everything from Bell's evangelical upbringing and his rise to fame in both the progressive and conservative Christian subculture of the early 2000s to how Bell's pastoral and theological evolution reflects the dichotomy at the heart of American Christianity generally and evangelicalism specifically: namely, that God is both "intimate companion and a wrathful judge." Sanneh fleshes out this tension by describing the ways in which prominent evangelical leaders responded to *Love Wins* and the inherent tension the book sought to unearth:

> In one sense, Bell followed the logic of evangelicalism to its conclusion: forced to choose between his personal Jesus and his perfect Bible, he chose Jesus, and set out to reexamine the

story he thought he knew. It is dangerous to be guided solely by your moral intuition, but surely it's no less dangerous to ignore it . . . even [Tim] Keller concedes that the evangelical idea of Hell is unsatisfyingly incomplete. In his view, some questions about the afterlife will have to wait until we get there. . . . This is a wise and gentle demurral, but it's also a profoundly unsettling view of God, who will seem "merciful and just" once we're dead—but not, apparently, until then.

As Sanneh's treatment winds to a close, it highlights the role Bell now occasionally plays in-between book tours and podcasts. He has become a sort of pastor for hire, re-creating a "miniature version of the thing he had just left behind: a church" with fifty retreat-goers (at the writing of Sanneh's article) in a conference room on the Southern California coast near Malibu. While pouring wine and breaking bread for each person in attendance, Bell does what he has likely done every week for the previous two decades of his life: serve communion to those gathered before him. When pressed by Sanneh on the not-so-subtle similarities between these small gatherings and the church he founded that was still meeting each week in the hollowed-out carcass of a defunct mall in Michigan, Bell quietly reminds us of the truth at the bottom of all faiths and families: "It's the most frustrating institution in the world . . . but when it's firing on all cylinders, there's absolutely nothing like it."

"WHAT THE WORLD NEEDS FROM US NOW"

If Christianity has anything left for us on the other side of desperate self-interest, it won't be found on the smoke-filled stage of a megachurch or the sold-out tour of a Christian blogger turned best-selling author. It will be found on the underside of this, our crumbling American empire.

In 2002, Bishop C. Vernie Russell made headlines when his congregation, Mount Carmel Baptist Church in Norfolk, Virginia, began hosting monthly debt liquidation revivals. During these meetings—amid the praying, singing, and sermonizing that typify most charismatic religious revivals—Mount Carmel would take up an offering. But instead of using it to pay the preacher, the church, or a mission agency, the church would "save" someone in the sanctuary from their debt. In the words of Bishop Russell, "They couldn't serve their master when they were busy serving MasterCard." At one point, the congregation had wiped out around $320,000 worth of debt.

Fast forward seventeen years and travel about two hundred miles south of Norfolk, and you'll find a similar story at Jubilee Baptist Church in Chapel Hill, North Carolina. Jubilee is a congregation that used to have a different name, Ephesus, and a bit of a different ethos in the years preceding the church's hiring of Kevin Georgas as its pastor. Before Georgas, Ephesus Baptist Church had dwindled to nineteen people—mostly senior adults and their caregivers. But thanks to a failed building plan, the congregation was debt-free, with an additional $600,000 in savings. Writing about Jubilee Baptist for Buzzfeed News in 2019, Anne Helen Petersen describes the conversation Georgas held with one longtime Ephesus member about the next steps following the deaths of several other longtime members, which left the church with just a handful of remaining congregants:

> With Ephesus down to 12 active members in 2018, Georgas sat down with Curtis Booker, and the existing leadership board of the church, and presented three options. One: Shut down, sell the property, and fund other nonprofits in town. Two: Find a young church that's meeting somewhere temporary, give them the building, and graft the remaining members onto that congregation. Three: Have conversations about what's been good at Ephesus, and not so good—and rebuild the church around, in Georgas's words, "what the world needs from us now." Georgas remembered Booker saying something that would stick with him: "For the longest time, I thought that faithfulness looked like carrying on what we've been given here. But maybe faithfulness looks like what my family did

when they started the church: making something new where
there wasn't anything before."

Turns out what the "world needs from us now" looks a lot like what
Bishop Russell found in Norfolk almost two decades earlier: saving
people from capitalism, from debt, and ultimately from the accompanying shame and failure of sinking. In this tension, Jubilee Baptist Church was born and would be committed, in their own words,
to loving "as if another world was possible." They do this through
monthly debt-liberation grants given to members of the church and
the creation of a jubilee fund, where money is directed toward lifting
"two to four people out of poverty in a given year." Amid much of the
rhetoric we often hear about the degrading effects of handouts, one
early Jubilee member describes the surprisingly difficult experience of
allowing the church to pay his debts despite being willing to pay
off the debts of other members: "'Last month we paid off the debt of
someone I knew, and I felt *nothing* but joy for them,' he explained.
'But I still feel like getting my own debt forgiven, it's a cop-out, and I
don't deserve it.'"

As the conversation between this congregant and Petersen continues, one thing becomes clear: talking about debt, about capitalism,
and about the resultant pain of trying to survive it all isn't political,
socialist, or progressive. It's human, *and* it's terribly Christian. "I asked
him what about the church made it feel different, and he told me that
he keeps thinking of the plot of Stephen King's *It*," Petersen reflects.
"'There are these kids who are being terrorized by an evil clown,' he
summarized, 'and the clown is just *kicking their asses*. But they eventually figure out that the clown's power is keeping them afraid and
divided. And as soon as they realized that, they knew how to fight
back. And I realized that that's what we're doing with the church:
We're beating the shit out of those evil clowns.'"

Richard Rohr once wrote that "what we know about God is
important, but what we do with what we know about God is even
more important." When the animating impulse behind Christianity is
mostly an effort in saving our own asses (as Job might put it), it will

only activate our individual and collective fight-or-flight response. This kind of Christian practice effectively shuts off any creative or thoughtful engagement with the world out of a desire to never die. (Enter the unfailing evangelical support of Donald Trump, stage right.) But when we read the story of God forward, with eyes remade for wonder, we can't help but encounter a God who self-disinterestedly dies for the salvation of everything and everyone—regardless of how anyone might eventually vote, live, love, and spend Sunday mornings. Reading Christianity forward—from a place of open-ended faith rather than fearful orthodoxy—radically reforms, reparents, and resurrects our view of what is possible, what is good, and what is ultimately true about ourselves, our world, and even our threadbare democracy.

The problem with this kind of approach is that it can't be boiled down to a faith statement, creed, or list of values on a church website. It requires a radical kind of trust that there is something that will eventually catch us and keep us afloat at the bottom of the slippery slope. Anxious orthodoxy won't ever do that. Believe me, I've tried.

The kind of God we meet in the midst of our aired pain reintroduces us to the truth that people are complicated, confusing, and sometimes desperate. But people are also almost always capable—*when they are themselves*—of remarkably loving, creative, and sacrificial acts of redemption. In the face of a God astride some wicked waves on the Sea of Galilee, Peter found it possible to rethink his own policies on late-night water-walking. In the face of dissolution, the aged parishioners of Ephesus Baptist felt it was time to "make something new."

I encounter this kind of resurrected creativity every day in my therapy office whenever I pause to ask questions about the family histories of my patients. In the midst of sometimes profound experiences with abuse, neglect, and abandonment at the hands of trusted loved ones, there remains an unconquerable, underlying impulse for most of us to give more than what we were given—even if it sometimes feels like the giving of this gift might destroy us. When fatherless fathers and motherless mothers who never received the trustworthy love they were owed bring new possibilities, emotional depth, and self-disinterested love into the lives of the kids they are now raising, it resurrects whole family trees. It re-creates the world. It is a kind of faith that stops fearing punishment and chasing reward. Despite capitalism's weaponizing of our self-interest, it's almost as if this resurrecting, self-disinterested impulse has somehow been baked into us. After all these years, I still tear up in its presence. Hearing my patients' stories, I am reminded that when I most wanted to die myself, I met a dying God who saved me even though she had chemo earlier that day.

The book of Job teaches us that when destructively entitled American folk religion gets its hands on your faith, it will only interrupt your pain, ignore your limp, explain away your questions, and strike up the Oscars band before your lament has had time to finish. American folk religion always starts at the end of the story, during the "making it" montage, where Jesus and his followers are all in on the joke. This makes it difficult for many of us American Christians to know what to do, exactly, with complicated folks like Job, or Tupac, or the depressed, or you, or the indebted, or your Republican uncle, or civil rights activists, or the grieving, or teen moms, or me, or LGBTQ pastors, or high schoolers yelling the F-word in algebra. American folk religion has no idea what to do with almost all of Jesus's closest followers as they fearfully locked themselves away in an upper room or headed down to the tomb to say goodbye one final time to the person who gave their lives gravity: "*But why are they hiding and crying? Don't they know they've already won!?*"

On the other hand, a Christianity willing to die for the world without expectation for reward, respect, or power is the last outpost of unconquered, unstandardized, and uncapitalized territory. No algorithm can explain why people who have never gotten what they were owed—from God, from their families, from the world, and even from the religion founded in Jesus's name—continue to self-disinterestedly love it and us anyway. Their sacrifice resurrects all of us.

If we'll let them, these disinterested prophets introduce us to a Christianity that doesn't save us by finally bringing our dreams to life but one that keeps us afloat even when those dreams sink again and again. Their kind of Christianity is a miserable failure. Sometimes it leaks. It swears when it drops a flashlight on its foot when the power suddenly goes out. It makes weird faces in family photos and gets uncomfortably honest about its breakups after too much wine at your cousin's wedding reception. This kind of faith sometimes seems like it's barely hanging on, but it never gives up, even when it has every reason to, even when it stops breathing for three days. This is a Christianity that brings newness to deadness, even if the newness was something we would never have chosen for ourselves. It's a newness that doesn't ride off into the sunset but that is coughing and screaming and gurgling and terrifying and scarred and limping and never quite whole but still standing nonetheless. That sort of Christianity? Well, it might just blow the doors off of the universe.

I guess you could say there *has* always been a slippery slope. But the point wasn't to climb up it but to slide down it. Instead of fearing, fighting, or continually fleeing from God and one another, it's time we died to what most of us in America have been taught to call Christianity. Instead of anxiously pursuing salvation to the detriment of ourselves, each other, and our world, it's time we died to that. Instead of internalizing the pain of disappointing the God of unyielding market growth and awesomeness, it's time we died to that too. And it's past time we allowed ourselves the gift of breaking bread, pouring wine, and communing with a mysterious, trustworthy, hashtagless God who sets a table for us to try to figure this thing out together, again and again and again.

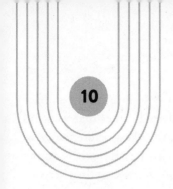

What If We Weren't Afraid of Each Other?

How to Be Complicated

> When I label people, I no longer have to deal with them thoughtfully. I no longer have to feel overwhelmed by their complexity, the lives they live, the dreams they have. I know exactly where they are inside—or forever outside—my field of care, because they've been taken care of. The mystery of their existence has been solved and filed away before I've had a chance to be moved by them or even begun to catch a glimpse of who they might be. They've been neutralized.
>
> —David Dark, *Life's Too Short*

For as long as I can remember, much of my extended family, at one time or another, identified as teetotalers: folks who abstain from alcohol consumption of any kind for religious (in my case, read "Southern Baptist") reasons. Historically, my people don't drink, dance (even at weddings), gamble, or curse.

Imagine my surprise, then, when I discovered an almost empty handle of gin under the kitchen sink while cleaning out my teetotaling

great-aunt's rancher after her death. This may seem a rather tame dis-
covery when compared to the eulogy delivered earlier that weekend
by her longtime Baptist pastor and friend who, just before the evan-
gelistic invitation, spun a few yarns about driving his mother and my
great-aunt to the casino one state over on the weekends. Everyone
knowingly chuckled. Everyone, I should say, but me.

The shocking thing wasn't necessarily my great-aunt's wild side
but that everyone handled it so well. It was like they had known about
all those slots and screwballs for years. As I later came to find out, they
had. Or, as my grandmother put it in response to my flabbergasted
questioning about her late sister's double life, "Eric, sometimes you
need to let off a little steam, but there's no reason to go on and on
about it." Cool. Where was this existential chillness when I was afraid
of being burned forever in a lake of molten lava with Satan and his
minions as a *fourth grader*?

The betrayal I felt was less about the life of my great-aunt, whom
we all called Mimi, and more that I had spent so much of my own
actually believing her words about God's judgment and the dangers
of alcohol and "the flesh." Her uncomplicated beliefs—which she and
many others in my family knowingly failed to practice—ended up
forming much of my own interior disposition toward the divine and
almost everything else (dancing included). This all-or-nothing belief
system taught me to internalize and take responsibility for the failures
of my own faith and for my struggle to grasp how exactly a human
might one day become, as Jesus commands, "perfect" as our "heavenly
Father is perfect" (Matthew 5:48).

Mimi's funeral introduced me to an organizing principle of evangelical Christianity, at least as it is often practiced by white people here
in the South: a judiciously maintained effort in disavowing the dichotomy between our actual lives and the expressed tenets of our faith. The
fruits of this Spirit often look like pretending, ignoring, covering up,
and hiding *in the name of God*. To be "perfect" in our tradition is an
effort in constantly managing our brand of socially acceptable moral
perfection at all costs (including, but not limited to, the hiding of
all the complicated parts of your life under the kitchen sink). Think

of this kind of faith as the world's first social media algorithm—an Instagram before Instagram—providing a way to tidily standardize, brand, and boil down the mysterious and complex areas of human life into things that are easily consumable by others for the sake of our God. What is white evangelicalism if not an effort to simultaneously hide *and* display your life so as to faithfully reveal how *this* religion actually changes you for the better, makes you happier, sands down all your rough edges, removes the power of your addictions, and heals your family with just one decision: to let Jesus become your Lord and Savior? *If only you would sign up for his mailing list today.*

You don't have to be a therapist to have heard stories about the pressure to perform, produce, and display "perfection" or "holiness" on Sundays that many people grew up with and internalized long before Zuckerberg started tracking our movements for marketers. Just like you don't have to have grown up white and Southern Baptist to imagine what it's like to feel like you are never beyond the gaze of a God constantly disappointed with last quarter's efforts.

Of course, everyone is imperfect, complicated, broken, and interesting. It's just that in my neck of the woods they have the good sense to do it *quietly*. Enter my bighearted, faithful, slot-playing, gin-drinking, Bible-thumping, teal-sweat-suit-wearing, teetotaling great-aunt. While working at the local health department for more than thirty years, tirelessly delivering medical services for indigent clients, she also bemoaned the "welfare state"—which allowed her to retire at sixty-five with a pension and access to health care—because "God helps those who help themselves, Eric."

My tradition may have instilled in me a love for the biblical text, faithfully serving my community, the nuances of Saint Paul's missionary journeys through Asia Minor, and the Welch's grape juice flowing through the veins of my Lord and Savior Jesus Christ when we took communion four times a year. But it never taught me how to be okay with my own and the world's profound inconsistencies. It never helped me become a person, because people are complicated, and our complexity was always discouraged as a detriment to our faith and our witness to the world. My inherited evangelical tradition showed me how to label, organize, and categorize all of life (both my own and others) as a sacred duty. This is good; they're bad; that's wrong; it's secular. But this? *This* is Christian. I was taught to take a Word that became flesh and blood, bone and sinew, Jewish and crucified, and turn it back into more words: a brand, a label, an algorithm underneath which we must all be sorted eternally. How one understands themselves according to this logic—this brand, really—is with a singular question: *Are you saved?*

Presumably this question is meant in the context of one's eternal destination, as discussed in the previous chapter, but this question can also serve as a kind of vetting for whether you understand yourself to be worthy of love and acceptance presently. "Are you a Christian?" is yet one more way of condensing life, people, faith, or even a God who became a human into something consumable that we can immediately accept or reject, love or condemn, believe in or doubt. David Dark calls this kind of distillation of our neighbors "a form of violence" in which we never allow ourselves to gracefully become—as I was by the life of my own great-aunt—"overwhelmed by their complexity."

But what if we could be overwhelmed? What if, instead of treating everyone around us as possible competitors, fearful of both their good fortune and our own failure, we collaborated with them? In a world where scarcity thoroughly sorts and separates us, what if our shared complexity could bring us back together? To find out, though, we may have to risk talking with people who hate us.

CONVERSATIONS WITH PEOPLE WHO HATE ME

"You know, when I said this to you, when I said you were a 'talentless hack,' I had never conversed with you in my life, really. I didn't really know anything really about you. And I think that a lot of times, that's what the comment sections really are, it's really a way to get your anger at the world out on random profiles of strangers, pretty much." These are the words of a man digital artist Dylan Marron identifies as "Doug" for a TED talk he gave in 2018 entitled "Empathy Is

Not Endorsement." Marron has racked up millions of views, comments, and interactions through his efforts at taking "complicated social issues," as he puts it, and working to find "accessible ways to talk about them through interviews, short-form videos and satire." Two such formats were his popular "Sitting in Bathrooms with Trans People," a bathroom-based interview series with trans individuals during the contentious rise of discriminatory "bathroom bills," and his "Every Single Word" series, where he edited down popular films to only the words spoken by people of color as a way of discussing representation in the entertainment industry. Naturally, because of Marron's rather wide internet reach, he's received quite of bit of what he calls "internet hate," in which he has been dismissed, disparaged, and frequently "dragged" by folks online.

Initially, Marron responded to the flood of vitriol by returning it blow for blow: "At first, I would screenshot their comments and make fun of their typos, but this soon felt elitist and ultimately unhelpful. So over time, I developed an unexpected coping mechanism." This "unexpected coping mechanism" was looking through the profile pictures, memes, posts, and digital content of those who took the time to troll him and eventually reaching out directly to ask one question: "Why did you write that?" Marron then cataloged these interviews in a series he playfully titled "Conversations with People Who Hate Me."

Marron found that when he began from a place of interest—by asking each person to tell him more about who they are—empathy suddenly emerged. Here's Marron explaining more about his experience: "Empathy, it turns out, is a key ingredient in getting these conversations off the ground, but it can feel very vulnerable to be empathizing with someone you profoundly disagree with. So I established a helpful mantra for myself. Empathy is not endorsement. . . . It just means that I'm acknowledging the humanity of someone who was raised to think very differently from me." While Marron acknowledges that there are limits to this kind of work—abuse, trauma, and safety being chief among them—and that empathy and conversation don't "radically heal a politically divided country and cure systemic injustice," his work does reveal a truth at the bottom of our often polarized selfhood: "Sometimes the most subversive thing you could do was to actually speak with the people you disagreed with, and not simply at them."

So much of our life now, especially online, finds itself sorted by an attention economy solely concerned with increasing our engagement with its product. One component of this great sorting process—in which we've all willingly signed away our personal data to be utilized—is the way that it truncates or eliminates human weirdness, not because this truncation is actually better for us, but because it's better for the platform. To make ourselves more searchable, more accessible, and more marketable, we actively participate in the disavowal of our own complexity. The constant draining of this complexity leaves us open to discomfiting targeted ads but also a kind of political partisanship destroying our democracy. Citing the work of political scientist Lilliana Mason, Ezra Klein describes the ways that our multifaceted human weirdness finds itself shoved into alignment by a hyperpartisanship Mason labels a "mega-identity." These partisan megaidentities then serve to explain every one of our choices—from where we buy groceries to where we live—as political ones and ultimately end up stoking an animosity toward one another that, according to Mason, is "unsupported by our [relatively minor] degrees of political disagreement."

However, as Marron reminds us, when our supposed enemies become fully human before us, they are suddenly suffused with a creative complexity that refuses to be controlled by the *in*humanity of the (digital and real) world around us. Once we begin empathetically communicating across our divides, we might find that those around us become something more interesting than just "random profiles of strangers," "trolls," "monsters," "Democrats," or "Republicans." The unconquerable and contradictory weirdness we often find in one another, rather than prolonging our alienation, is, in fact, one of the last remaining ways in which we are able to transcend the co-opting, standardizing, and polarizing of our lives for financial and politically motivated reasons. "I imagine one of the reasons people cling to their hates so stubbornly," James Baldwin once mused, "is because they sense, once hate is gone, they will be forced to deal with pain."

The pain and angst that made us and that we have occasionally unleashed upon one another connect us to a foundational truth about being a person. We are always more interesting than our worst moments and our greatest successes.

MULTIDIRECTED PARTIALITY

Following the 2020 election, author Rebecca Solnit penned a passionate plea for the newly victorious Democratic Party to stop making efforts at "meeting Nazis halfway" in their policy decisions and public rhetoric out of a misguided loyalty to some "hopelessly naive version of centrism." She argues that "this inanity is also applied to the questions of belief and fact and principle, with some muddled cocktail of moral relativism and therapists' 'everyone's feelings are valid' applied to everything. But the truth is not some compromise halfway between the truth and the lie, the fact and the delusion, the scientists and the propagandists. And the ethical is not halfway between white supremacists and human rights activists, rapists and feminists, synagogue massacrists and Jews, xenophobes and immigrants, delusional transphobes and trans people. Who the hell wants unity with Nazis until and unless they stop being Nazis?"

Solnit's article would prove incredibly prescient, as Republicans loyal to Donald Trump violently stormed the Capitol during the ratification of Joe Biden's victory almost two months later. Five people—and an entire country's confidence in democracy—died during the attempted insurrection.

In their book *Between Give and Take: A Clinical Guide to Contextual Therapy*, Ivan Boszormenyi-Nagy and Barbara Krasner describe a therapeutic stance they term "multidirected partiality." This kind of approach occurs whenever a therapist is able to generously enter into and seek to understand the complicated, complex, and painful feelings that each member of an aggrieved family system is entitled to, no matter the amount of pain that individual may have wreaked on others over the course of his or her life. Boszormenyi-Nagy and Krasner argue that radical empathy and perspective-taking on the part of the therapist create opportunities for all members of a family to eventually understand that the pain inflicted upon them was done not by a "meritless monster" but by another complicated human being who "has himself suffered as a childhood victim."

While multidirected partiality might, at first blush, appear to fall victim to what Solnit terms a "muddled cocktail of moral relativism and therapists' 'everyone's feelings are valid' applied to everything," it is not a poorly employed therapeutic effort at sweeping pain under the rug. Instead, multidirected partiality holds us in the presence of our own and others' complexity long enough to be made accountable to the kind of pain we have experienced and the kind of pain we have unleashed in response. We all have blood on our hands. Admitting this doesn't undermine what we are entitled to. Nor does it tidily explain away the violent behavior of others.

Multidirected partiality simply invites us to slow down in the face of deep pain and to begin a fresh conversation about what we owe one another and are owed *by* one another. Don't be confused; peace isn't the goal of Boszormenyi-Nagy and Krasner's work. Justice, equity, and increasing understanding are. "People take time," David Dark writes. "But in our haste, we size them up or cut them down to what we take to be a more manageable size, labeling people instead of trying to hear, understand or welcome them. . . . It's as if we'll do anything to avoid the burden of having to think twice."

Turning our enemies into monsters is a far too easy and convenient explanation for our pain, and it's also counterproductive. Monsters can't apologize, can't change, and can't give us what we are owed because they are incapable of being anything other than monsters. Even if our justifiable rage feels incredible when it comes pouring out of us, reflexive, dehumanizing shame and retributive violence fossilize unhelpful, abusive, or monstrous behavior within those who owe us better. Social media is so frequently unhelpful for our polarized democracy because digital vitriol and righteous indignation turn people into "random profile pictures" or "problems" rather than actual humans, with problematic behaviors and beliefs formed by problematic family, economic, and political systems. Empathy isn't turning a blind eye toward abuse or monstrous behavior; it's an act of nonanxiously holding people responsible for what they did to us by returning them to their own humanity. Only humans can apologize; monsters—or should I say Nazis—never will. That is, until they stop being Nazis.

In an interview with the *New York Times*, civil rights leader, feminist icon, and professor Loretta J. Ross describes a class she teaches at Smith College to help students engage in an act of "calling in" their political and ideological opponents rather than tirelessly calling them out. Calling in holds people accountable to their humanity without bypassing their complexity because we find their actions offensive. "It's a call out done with love" and frequently involves directly communicating with the offender in person or on an actual phone call rather than simply feeding them to the internet's insatiable need for negative content. "I think we overuse that word 'trigger' when really we mean discomfort," Ross argues. "And we should be able to have uncomfortable conversations."

Professor Ross recalls a comment from her supervisor at the Center for Democratic Renewal, Rev. C. T. Vivian: "When you ask people to give up hate, you have to be there for them when they do." In response, Ross has given her life to this work, as she accompanied reformed Ku Klux Klan members and white supremacists across America in their efforts to make atonement and restitution for the pain they caused. As the interview draws to a close, Ross gives a final word: "We have a saying in the movement: Some people you can work with and some people you can work around. But the thing that I want to emphasize is that the calling-in practice means you always keep a seat at the table for them if they come back." To these Baptist ears, that sounds like communion.

When we allow our abusers, our parents, our political opponents, or our enemies to think we believe them to be monstrous, evil, or "baskets of deplorables," it postpones both their reckoning and our own resurrection. Labels forged in the fires of our fear and pain will only subjugate us, abuse us, and dehumanize us by turning us into little more than the worst thing we have done or failed to do. All of us are more than that. Without regular, cellular reminders of complexity—which so frequently elude us in a world of anxious competition and tidy, digital standardization—we are in danger of sacrificing one another on the altar of the Black Friday sale we've been taught to call normal life in America.

The kind of partiality I'm describing does not ask us to expose ourselves to further victimization or abuse at the hands of unsafe family members, friends, bosses, and even whole institutions. Despite the popular theology of my inherited religious tradition as it concerns wives married to abusive husbands or children raised by abusive parents, our death or continual mistreatment won't save or fix those who have wielded violence against us. Since we never deserved their mistreatment, surviving it now won't ever be an act of grace toward them. This is because our mistreatment isn't about us at all; it is about something that predates us, a pain that continues to trickle down upon all of us. When we persist in toxic and abusive relationships (online and in person) out of a belief that we somehow owe it to the relationship, to God, to the kids, or to the person whose hand and words are raised against us, it is one more manifestation of a destructive entitlement that flows unabated generation to generation. Multidirected partiality seeks to understand and interrupt the pain of those who would abuse us, not by allowing their abuse to continue, but as an act of resistance to a system that has and will continue abusing all of us.

Holding others accountable for their own complicated humanity by nonviolently and passionately asserting our own—this is a form of creative resistance in a world demanding efficient standardization, organized polarization, and ready competition. Leaving the door cracked an inch or so on the humanity of those who have harmed us is a truly subversive effort. It requires slowing down our immediately activated fight-or-flight response to pain, trauma, and internet trolls. Rather than constantly fearing or fighting the humans around us, asking about who these people are, the stories that raised them, and the pain that continues to haunt them today is how, as Marron attests, empathy bubbles up. Empathy is not an endorsement for what they've done, but empathy does endorse and empower who they *are*: a person with a story, not a brand, profile, competitor, or even a troll.

There is this benedictory reminder underneath the noise and toothless cancelations of American capitalism: empathy, rather than betraying our weakness and fear, is actually a source of strength. When used effectively, empathy frees us from what has possessed us, trapped us, and kept us alienated from ourselves and one another. It's time our complexity brought us back together.

COMMUNIONISM

A few years ago, a good friend of mine reminded me that the Bible wasn't originally written in the King's English. So when Jesus invites us to become "perfect" like our heavenly Father in Matthew 5:48, the word "perfect" is actually the Greek word *teleios*, which generally communicates the idea of something being completed or "needing nothing further for completeness." A better translation (put forth by both Greek philosophers and early Christians) might read, "*Be complete, therefore, as your heavenly Father is complete.*"

Even the word for "perfect" in Hebrew, Jesus's religious mother tongue, is the word *shalom*, which, loosely translated, connotes this same sense of peace, completeness, and at-home-ness with the world. Be complete, be okay, be at peace with a complicated world, therefore, as your heavenly parent is complete, okay, and at peace with a complicated world.

This translation makes even more sense in light of this verse's actual location in a much larger collection of some of Jesus's most well-known and radical teachings known as the Sermon on the Mount. Throughout this sermon, Jesus commands his disciples to make space for enemies at their own tables, welcome and love people who can't pay them back for that love, and live in solidarity with a complex and sometimes violent world even if it kills them in the process. As one verse from earlier in his teachings reminds us, "[God] makes his sun rise on the evil and on the good, and sends rain on the righteous and on the unrighteous" (Matthew 5:45). When it rains, in the world Jesus is envisioning, everyone gets wet.

Several years after his sermon, the apostle Paul picks up on Jesus's self-sacrificing impulse by invoking the idea of communion as a way to bring the ragged and polarized community of early Christians in Corinth back together. Here, Paul is angrily blogging *at* the Corinthians from the nearby city of Ephesus: "For I received from the Lord what I also handed on to you, that the Lord Jesus on the night when he was betrayed took a loaf of bread, and when he had given thanks, he broke it and said, 'This is my body that is for you. Do this in remembrance of me'" (1 Corinthians 11:23–24). Paul ends the paragraph rather ominously: "Examine yourselves, and only then eat of the bread and drink of the cup. For all who eat and drink without discerning the body, eat and drink judgment against themselves. For this reason many of you are weak and ill, and some have died" (1 Corinthians 11:28–30). It seems Paul is arguing that these Corinthian Christians find themselves weak, ill, and even dead thanks to their inability to eat the communion meal, together, without it becoming one more Christian practice undermined by social class, ethnicity, and theology.

After serving his disciples a final meal where he invites them to reflect on the bread and wine of his body and blood, Jesus notes the existence of a betrayer among the disciples whose "hand is on the table" (Luke 22:21). Jesus is eating with someone who sold him out, and he knows it. It's almost impossible for the earliest Christians not to become disconnected, confused, and even willing to betray one another (including the aforementioned Son of God) for money, power, and salvation. Just like it's almost impossible for Christians in the twenty-first century not to become disconnected, confused, and even willing to betray one another (including the aforementioned Son of God) for money, power, and salvation. Being a human is hard, even when God and his favorite grumpy blogger are right there across the table from you.

As I've gotten older, though, and survived more than a few contentious elections, Thanksgiving dinners, and seemingly unending global pandemics, I have come to realize that the Last Supper isn't some boring intro Christians pay lip service to in order to remember some *other* miraculous and hard-to-swallow part of Jesus's life. Communion *is* the hard-to-swallow part. The fact that a God (which is what many Christians believe Jesus to be) could stand to be misunderstood to the point of death by twelve people who would then be responsible to carry on his work after he was gone—well, it is beyond comprehension. A few towns over, in Babylon, they believed their God had literally created the earth by ripping another monster in two (it's an awesome story). In America, some people once believed their God had all the words—especially the best ones. And in that rented room two thousand years ago in Jerusalem, before the dry ice and laser lights of resurrection, we find out that the Christian God is surprisingly okay with people missing the point about who he is and what he's here to do. It seems like God even sort of expects it. One of this God's followers even goes so far as to turn him in to the authorities as a political criminal, and yet there Jesus is, supping with him all the same.

Perhaps, then, Jesus's request for his followers to "do this"—commune over bread and wine—wasn't an invitation to hermetically seal his words and actions behind professionalism, denominational theology, socioeconomic status, and traditionalism. What if, instead, the "do this" is an invitation for humanity to do things that ground us in the shared witness of our complexity and pain without it killing us? When Christianity regularly introduces us to complicated humans sitting across from us—people we otherwise have no business knowing—it is an elemental, sacramental reminder that we all live on bread and wine. Even when we have different political and theological ideas that cause us to sell Jesus out again and again, we all still hunger and thirst. We all still experience pain and deliver pain in response. We're human, and we're complicated. And in the presence of our great complexity, Jesus just keeps breaking himself open and pouring himself out again and again.

To be clear, *we* aren't the ones submitting ourselves to the possibility of exploitation or abuse or sacrifice at the communion table; *God* is. God risks God's own selfhood, reputation, glory, and power to bring us back together, even if it kills God in the process—because that's what real parents do. Real parents take responsibility for the well-being of their family at all costs, even if it kills them in the process.

To acknowledge the radical and unpopular nature of this kind of dinner, we might be better served by changing its rather tepid title from the "Lord's Supper," as I was taught to call it, to something more fitting: *communionism*. Like multidirected partiality, communionism subverts our commitment to self-interest, fear, and competition by bringing us face-to-face with other complicated humans across tradition, political identity, geography, theology, socioeconomic status, ethnicity, and what Paul later called "the dividing wall of hostility" in order to bring a whole new world into being—*together*. Not in the name of tongue-bitten peace, theological orthodoxy, or tradition, but in the name of a misunderstood and executed God who loves her kids more than her own glory.

When this God shares a table with us, even though we sold her out and put her to death, it resurrects not only us, individually, but our families, our communities, and our world. The gods who raised us and refuse to die, refuse to risk the devaluation of their own glory, and refuse to be undone and replaced—these gods cannot bring us resurrection. They can't even host Thanksgiving dinner without yelling about politics and your sister's new nose ring. Only when these old gods die can we finally look one another in the eye and bear the weight of our responsibility to break bread and pour wine in the presence of complicated, limping, but surprisingly trustworthy love.

"I don't think I believe in God anymore," a teenager once quietly confessed to me when I was on a staff at a Southern Baptist youth camp. During our conversation, I discovered that this teenager's parents had gotten divorced over the previous year, and she had just escaped an abusive relationship before coming to camp. "That's okay,"

I whispered, "sometimes I don't either. But I try to keep in mind that God already died and came back to life once. So chances are if we're dealing with a God worth believing in, this God will probably show up again whether or not we keep believing."

If your church, your religious tradition, your economic theory, or your political identity cannot entertain its own end as a way of bringing something greater, healthier, and more complete into the world, then it is, in my old Southern Baptist parlance, an idol. If some allegiance of yours cannot contemplate its own end, it's a false god, a kind of hokey magic we use to control fear and uncertainty, even if we know, deep down, *it's total bullshit.* For instance, I used to believe that God would kill you forever in a lake of fire if you didn't unfailingly believe in his goodness and mercy. This kind of contradictory, self-interested fear provided clarity to the way I lived, to the way I loved other people (or didn't), and to the way I ordered almost every facet of my existence. But it almost killed me.

In the wake of this God's death, I have discovered that all of us must live in the world we work to create. Our churches are entitled to keep existing, our denominations are entitled to keep existing, our social media networks are entitled to keep existing, our movements for justice are entitled to keep existing, and Christianity itself is entitled to keep existing insofar as they selflessly pump love and trustworthiness into an atmosphere of anxiety, scarcity, pain, and partisanship parading as truth. These things don't get to exist simply because they already exist and have buildings, bank accounts, and founding documents. So did the Roman Empire, the Branch Davidians, and Enron. When four-year-olds are jailed at our southern border, a sitting president has actively campaigned against democracy, millions have died from Covid-19, Black and brown people are regularly killed by the police, and the Arctic Circle has hit eighty degrees, it's time to find out why exactly the world needs our packed "worship centers," on the one hand, or our sparsely populated sanctuaries, on the other.

BEARING *WITHNESS*

Whenever our religious communities are formed by a self-disinterested faith in a self-disinterested God—instead of their own survival—they increase our capacity for complexity, creativity, and hopefulness. These kinds of communities happen within the context of communionism; in the presence of a flesh-and-blood encounter with hope and unexpected *difference* in the eyes and ears of another person sitting across from us, praying over us, and willing to be wrong *with* and *because of* an encounter with us. David Dark calls it "bearing *with*ness," and early Christians called it "incarnation." Rather than haggling over the reality of a disembodied God with specious technical rhetoric for all eternity, the flesh and blood of Jesus bring us face-to-face with a God who refuses to be defined, polarized, or algorithmized. Jesus introduces us to God in the flesh and not God in the faith statement.

If our own gatherings of contradictory, complicated, and politically co-opted humans can begin existing together in the tension of our differences without these differences destroying us in the process, it begs the question, *What else could we do together?*

One thing that still tethers me to church is the miracle of what happens when people—for no apparent reason—return to the source of what they were owed but never received from their parents, from life, and from God. When these people choose to give others the very things and experiences they were entitled to, with no expectation for reward, they are reparenting a world out of control. When LGBTQ people don clerical collars, stoles, or ripped jeans in order to preach in a church that has so frequently rejected them, they are reparenting a world out of control. When fatherless fathers and motherless mothers give to their own children a love and trustworthiness they never received themselves, they are reparenting a world out of control. When Black and brown people embody unconquerable selfhood, dignity, and prophetic resistance to a country and a Christian religious tradition that has so frequently overseen their enslavement and violent suppression, they are reparenting a world out of control. When construction workers and bowlers and bartenders and doctors and scholars and bloggers refuse to perpetuate a competitive and dehumanizing capitalist ethos by collaboratively creating cultures where humans take days off, use all of their sick leave, and refuse to become brands, they are reparenting a world out of control.

Anytime we bear the weight of another's complexity—without rushing to judgment, shame, or fear—bend down in their presence, and ask them their names and where they come from, we are reparenting a world out of control.

When my thoughts turn to what it's like to be complicated, I tearfully remember Mimi. And as I reflect upon the life of my great-aunt, it isn't the contradictory religiosity that dominates my memories. It's that she possessed this teetotaling faith in *me*, a cynical, acne-prone, and sullen adolescent boy from a divorced family trying, often unsuccessfully, to find his groove in the world. Mimi never let me believe that my limping imperfections, near-constant self-doubt, and exhausting cynicism were anything but a gift and a welcome friend to the divine (even though she would never have said something weird like "the divine").

Despite what she may have believed about God's preferences for how people spend their food stamps, how the world began, how it will end, or to which political party God always sends tax-deductible donations, she picked me up from school and listened to me complain about how alone I often felt. She was simply there, idling in her green Buick Regal, always on time, always fully present, sweat suit and all. The *with*ness of her complexity saved me back then, and it still saves me today.

In the face of inconsistency (both theological and existential), her trustworthy love for me made her perfect, grounded, and complete. I hope one day trustworthy love will do the same for me and for you whenever we find ourselves in the presence of someone who goes by the name Legion. As Saint Paul and John Lennon sort of put it, in the end all we have (or need) is love. Not right beliefs, not moral perfection, not political power, not even the rhetorical high ground—nothing but incarnate, complicated, trustworthy, flesh-and-blood love makes it out of this thing alive. It's time we trusted this love to do its job. It's time we trusted this love to hold us up and to let us float when we most feel like drowning—because it can, it has, and it will.

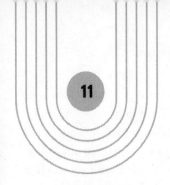

Why the Jar Is Always Smaller Than the Sky

May a space to daydream and slow down open to you. May you realize the power of taking rest since no one will give it to you. This is why rest is a resistance and a slow meticulous love practice. We must continue deprogramming from grind culture. We must continue not turning away from our own terror. We must deconstruct around the ways we uphold grind culture, capitalism and white supremacy. We must wake up. We will rest.

—Tricia Hersey, "Slowly Emerging after a 3 Week Sabbath"

One of the worst things that could have happened during late elementary school was someone finding out you still watched *Mister Rogers' Neighborhood*. I spent the majority of third grade loudly telling classmates that Jean Claude Van Damme's 1993 smash hit *Hard Target* was my favorite movie. John Woo's cinematic brilliance aside, my interest in Van Damme's work was linked to two key factors: (1) *Hard Target* was rated R, and (2) I had managed to witness a full twenty-five minutes of it from behind the loveseat in my parents' living room after sneaking out of bed. To be fair to Woo, though, I *did* catch an iconic scene involving Van Damme staring down unconscionable odds as he avoids a rain of bullets on an interstate overpass under construction.

Hard Target would become a liability later that year, though, as I wound up in the principal's office following a playground altercation where I may have called my friend John a "bastard" and shoved him to the ground, à la Van Damme. Let the record show that at the time I did not know what a "bastard" was. Thanks to Principal Williams's phone call to my mom, I still do today.

Just try letting slip your love of hand-stitched puppets, trolleys, kindly postal workers, and fifteen-minute discussions on death and haircuts with a cardiganed man in his midfifties to *this* elementary schooler. He just called someone a bastard, and his parents are divorced.

As you can probably guess, I grew up thinking Mister Rogers was terribly weak. In my family, his name regularly served as an insult. To be like Mister Rogers was to be overly soft or naive, and I am ashamed to admit that these thoughts persisted into my early thirties. It wasn't until the release of Morgan Neville's 2018 documentary *Won't You Be My Neighbor?* that I began to reconsider my stance on Rogers's legacy. The following year, 2019, Rogers experienced a thorough American canonization by having national treasure Tom Hanks portray him for Marielle Heller's *A Beautiful Day in the Neighborhood*. With his story in the able hands of Heller and Hanks, I found myself walking the aisle, so to speak, in the presence of Rogers's legacy.

In the film, we meet Rogers through the lens of cynical new-dad reporter Lloyd Vogel, whose editor has commissioned him to inter-view Rogers for *Esquire*. Vogel is a fictionalization of actual *Esquire* reporter Tom Junod, who famously profiled Rogers for the magazine in 1997 and titled his piece "Can You Say . . . Hero?" In the movie, as Vogel grapples with the parentification, destructive entitlement, and trickle-down pain of his struggles with becoming a father while being estranged from his own father, he meets Fred Rogers. The rest, they say, is history. Or when they're writers for *Esquire*, they say *this* instead:

> What is grace? I'm not certain; all I know is that my heart felt like a spike, and then, in that room, it opened and felt like an

umbrella. I had never prayed like that before, ever. I had always been a great prayer, a powerful one, but only fitfully, only out of guilt, only when fever and desperation drove me to it . . . and it hit me, right then, with my eyes closed, that this was the moment Fred Rogers—Mister Rogers—had been leading me to from the moment he answered the door of his apartment in his bathrobe and asked me about Old Rabbit. Once upon a time, you see, I lost something, and prayed to get it back, but when I lost it the second time, I didn't, and now this was it, the missing word, and the unuttered promise, the prayer I'd been waiting to say a very long time.

The world is, quite often, a terrible place. I spent the first five chapters of this book outlining how most of us maintain, organize, and ultimately internalize all this terribleness. I believe capitalism is certainly to blame, but so is the internet, so are our families, and so are we. Like I mentioned earlier, we all have to live in the world we work to create, and the one we've been raised in and continue to build remains uncreative and exhausting. It's literally killing us and everything else.

Whether we call the resultant internalized pain of this world depression or anxiety, grinding or branding, helicopter parenting or burning out, much like a four-year-old we've been ignoring for the better part of the afternoon, *the pain always gets our attention*. But to do so, the pain must get louder, and *louder*, and LOUDER until we ultimately wheel around and scream at it to pull itself together or go back to its room if it can't calm down. "Pain is unrelenting. It will get our attention," Brené Brown warns. "Despite our attempts to drown it in addiction, to physically beat it out of one another, to suffocate it with success and material trappings, or to strangle it with our hate, pain will find a way to make itself known."

For much of my life, I didn't have language for a world where we are treated the way we all deserve to be treated as kids. There is a wholly miraculous quality to the experience of having someone empathically get down on one knee, kindly look us in the eye, and, like Jesus on the shores of Gerasene, ask us our names and actually wait for the answer. This kind of treatment works to unclench our jaws, opens us up, and quite often ends up exorcizing whatever has been wreaking havoc inside of us for years now, even if it goes by "Legion." In the presence of a fuller accounting of Mister Rogers's work, attention, and unassuming selfhood, I found my own heart, as Junod puts it, suddenly opening up "like an umbrella."

I began seeing Mister Rogers not as naive, boring, or irrelevant but as prophetically *alive* in all the ways that tragicomic hip-hop and liberation theology are but in penny loafers. Fred Rogers was radically okay—with himself, with you, and with me. And his radical okayness seemed to make room for everyone else's to bubble up in his quiet presence. In a world where our collective resting heart rate is busyness and growth, this kind of quiet presence seems like an actual super-power, even if it *is* on PBS in the middle of the day.

As a newly minted convert in Rogers's celluloid congregation, I found myself then wondering, what if I had this superpower too? What if you and I and the rest of us were okay in the way Fred Rogers was? Like, on purpose, unapologetically, and unselfconsciously? What kind of world might open up before us if we patiently bear radical *with*ness to children of divorce, cynical reporters, and our own unacknowledged, internalized pain? What might start happening if we stopped the flow of destructive entitlement and parentification by giving our partners, our enemies, our friends, and the children around us a message that they cannot outrun, outgrow, or outgun our love? What might change in our families, in our churches, in our communities, and even in our own bodies if we started believing that God is more like Mister Rogers than some Badass Jean Claude Van Damme Jesus?

You may be thinking, "Won't living this way, like Jesus or Fred Rogers, leave us taken advantage of, hurt, abused, abandoned, or more likely to fall victim to some Pollyanna line about kindness in the face of unending bullet fire and bastards? Isn't this all kind of soft and vague—or worse, just another mandate that we should 'smile more' during the apocalypse? Life is R-rated, Eric. You have cuss words in this book; *don't patronize me.*"

I get that, which is why I don't talk my psychotherapy patients out of their pain, depression, or anxiety. Instead, I ask them to wait, to listen to their own breathing and their own heart beating for a moment, to lean into the complexity and wonder of a life brimming over with both barbarity and beauty. And upon sitting together, as nonanxiously as possible within the tension of it all, my patients and I find we aren't drowning. Instead, we both quietly realize that we are now, currently, floating together in the truth that we aren't yet dead, that our tombs are empty, and that maybe something new can still be brought into the world, broken as it is.

REST IS RESISTANCE

Rabbi Abraham Joshua Heschel once described the Sabbath, or the spiritual practice of ceasing from all work once a week, in a similar way. Heschel understood the Sabbath as the creation not of a particularly sacred space or institution or theological system within which God might regularly be found but of a "holiness in time." He says, "To gain control of the world of space is certainly one of our tasks. The danger begins when in gaining power in the realm of space we forfeit all aspirations in the realm of time. There is a realm of time where the goal is not to have but to be, not to own but to give, not to control but to share, not to subdue but to be in accord. Life goes wrong when the control of space, the acquisition of things of space, becomes our sole concern."

Whatever your spiritual tradition may be, I would argue that all humans are offered an opportunity to experience the kind of "holiness" (or buoyancy) Heschel describes. This kind of holiness won't ever be found solely within doctrines or particular spaces because it is constantly contained in time itself. You can't make it or build it or buy it because it's always around us. Sabbath is a way of inhabiting our bodies long enough to be made aware of possibilities available to us on the other side of productivity, ownership, and desperate dog-paddling. For Heschel, this tradition is born out of a foundational understanding of God as one who, after creating the world, took a nap and who, after freeing slaves from Egypt, reminded them to revere their day off each week with a kind of seriousness typically reserved for more important commandments like not murdering one another. Heschel is teaching us that this kind of rest isn't confined to a church or a day of the week but is constantly available to us whenever we remember to float. Sabbath is a regular invitation to interrupt our anxious and often fruitless efforts at owning the world rather than simply loving it and being loved by it.

"Rest is a form of resistance because it disrupts and pushes back against capitalism and white supremacy," writes community organizer, theologian, performance artist, and author Tricia Hersey, known as the "Nap Bishop." In her groundbreaking work as founder of the Nap Ministry, Hersey installs what she describes as "sacred and safe spaces for the community to rest together." Online and in person, Hersey advocates for the "liberating power of naps" that allows communities to resist internalized capitalism and "grind culture" by collectively opposing the dehumanization of self, others, and the earth. This is because sleep deprivation, Hersey notes, is a "racial and social justice issue." When Black and brown labor, wealth, and well-being have been continually stolen as a necessary by-product for the flourishing of our American economy, the act of people of color resting together— claiming their sacred birthright as children of a napping God—is prophetic resistance and an invitation for collective healing.

"Caring for myself is not self-indulgence," Audre Lorde famously teaches us in her final collection of essays and poetry, "it is self-preservation, and that is an act of political warfare." Black rest is a form of reparation. It represents a rightful reclamation of what was stolen by capitalist self-interest and racism. I can't speak about what it means for Black and brown Americans themselves to rest in public as a collective witness to their unconquerable dignity and worth. But I can tell you as a burned-out white guy checking work email on the weekends that Black rest teaches me how to nonviolently and creatively claim for myself a kind of Sabbath holiness, a kind of radical okayness, that has always been mine, and yours, and ours independently of what kind of profit our bodies can produce.

Rest is indeed resistance because it resurrects us and helps us reenvision what's possible. Like Mister Rogers and the Sabbath practices of ancient Near Eastern Hebrews, Lorde and Hersey introduce to us a kind of rest that invites us to trustfully lie down, to cease frantically swimming and just float awhile until we feel ready to rise once more and put our feet back on solid ground. These prophets don't rest only when the fight for justice is finally finished. Like Jesus in the stormy Sea of Galilee, they nap right in the middle of the struggle.

Only when we learn to rest—to float—can we muster the kind of creative energy required to imaginatively respond (rather than react) to the chaos of the world and the rising waves around us. Rest opens our eyes to what's been right in front of us the whole time. Rest returns us to where we were just eight hours earlier but with fresh eyes and a renewed appreciation for our own complexity and the complexity constantly buzzing around us.

YEAH, BUT HAVE YOU SEEN THEM PLAY ELKMONT?

I've always loved lightning bugs. Few things are more captivating to a nine-year-old in jean shorts from Sears than a creature whose hind end lights up an oppressively humid night sky like the erratically used brake lights on his grandfather's beige Lincoln Town Car. When you remember that this kid is an American raised on Nickelodeon, it makes sense that his default setting in the face of something mysterious and wonderful is to reach for the nearest commercial-sized pickle jar in order to corral this blinking sentry behind glass.

After catching said lightning bugs, I would fashion at least four air holes in the lid of the pickle jar before triumphantly placing it above my bed, like you might the stuffed head of a felled buck. I drilled those air holes knowing full well that by early morning, *my* lightning bugs (as they would now be eternally known) would be lying lifelessly in the bottom of a jar that once held sweet dill chips. It's strange to wield the power of a god at such a young age.

Years later, thanks to my lifelong affinity for these majestic creatures, some friends of mine were kind enough to invite me to the Elkmont campground in the Great Smoky Mountains National Park. There, after a short hike, I was able to view the synchronized flickering of millions of mating lightning bugs in early June. Despite having grown up exactly 51.8 miles away, I had never witnessed the "synchronous fireflies," as they are officially known. Soon thereafter, I became like your friend who has seen every band live, rudely interrupting folks noticing a few discrete flies buzzing in their yard at a cookout with, "Yeah, yeah, but have you seen them play Elkmont?" As much as it pains me to agree with your friend, sometimes you do, in fact, just have to be there.

This revelatory experience, I soon found, isn't unique to my interactions with lightning bugs, but it *is* sacred. In the midst of a life spent desperately attempting to own, define, and control a world beyond understanding, moments like what I witnessed at Elkmont tap me on the shoulder and confront me with an unavoidable truth: *the jar is always smaller than the sky.* What I mean is that the complexity flickering around all of us—the beauty and weirdness of our shared humanity—is bottomless whenever we stop trying to explain it, own it, or control it. Whenever we allow the strangeness and eccentricity of the lives flickering around us to deepen our appreciation for the wonder of being alive, it unlocks the door to what kind of world—what kind of synchronized movements—might be possible on the other side of our deadening self-interest and alienated conformity.

In moments that leave the hair on the backs of our necks upright, we are brought face-to-face with something bigger than productivity, bottomless growth, hyperventilating excess, and the internalized shame we have learned to quietly bear. That thing is unadulterated, unconquerable, unowned, and yet still synchronized light. It isn't just mine and it isn't just yours and it isn't just God's, because it's *ours* together. It's a trinity, a communal experience of oneness. We're made of it. It's in us and between us and around us. It predates us and yet outlives us. If we attempt to own it, name it, leverage it, organize it, and save it for later, we cease trusting and allowing it to be what it was always meant to be—which is part of something bigger than a jar on our bedside table. It can't save just me or you; that's not how the light works. It only saves all of us or none of us.

Becoming ourselves—becoming radically okay in the midst of our crumbling American empire—is like stumbling into a forest of lightning bugs when we've spent the whole of our lives trying to trap one or two in pickle jars. It's hard not to yell, "Why didn't anyone tell me this is happening so close to where I live!?" Radical okayness doesn't ignore the turmoil or avoid what makes life difficult; it simply realizes that working harder to own more of what has always been ours to enjoy together is a feeble kind of existence. Radical okayness acknowledges that there *is* a slippery slope, but the point wasn't to keep trying to climb up it, like a pyramid, but to slide down it, to rest at the bottom of it. Radical okayness isn't a well-adorned jar of a few asphyxiated fireflies on their last legs; it's a forest full of living ones.

When we're radically okay, we can do something more interesting than offer yet more jars of dead fireflies and self-interested religious noise in the face of chaotic desperation. This kind of freedom, on the other side of self-interested fear and scarcity, allows us to begin nonanxiously bending down, looking other humans in the eyes, empathically asking their names, and trustworthily offering them a chance to return to the truth of our shared humanity. Radical okayness stabilizes us, and it gives us the ability to reparent a world that never parented us in ways we deserved. It trusts that something other than naked self-interest pulls us up when we begin sinking. Like a good night's sleep, radical okayness reminds us that we have agency, that we are the adults now, and we don't have to keep doing this to one another. When we do finally eat, rest, and return to the truth of our shared complexity, together, who knows what new thing might happen next?

The ancients called this posture "priestly" or "sacred" because it gives language, shape, and voice—incarnation, really—to what God is like and to what kind of life is possible when we slow down long enough to consider the reality of its existence. Good religion, as Rabbi

Kushner reminds us, isn't about what happens in the future or in some other realm beyond this one for the benefit of God; it's about the kind of wonder happening all around us, where we are right now. Like Fred Rogers and napping in public, this kind of radical okayness may at first appear naive, boring, goofy, or humbly stooped. But like a tree blown almost parallel to the ground by high winds, it refuses to be broken. Despite the onslaught of wind and rain, these trees continue to convert the carbon dioxide of shame, scarcity, and bottomless burnout into more grace, more peace, and more oxygen. These trees survive and give life only because their roots run deep, to the source of what was owed to them by the world coming before them and to what they now owe the world coming after them.

When people are radically okay, they are adults, but not in the R-rated sense of the word. They are religious, but not in the self-interested sense of the word. They are saved, but not at the expense of others. They are whole, present, and complete, but not at the expense of themselves. Instead of grinding up or burning out everyone else like a perfectly curated Instagram brand, their radical okayness inspires us, fills us with joy, and brings us into the presence of something holy. This is what it's like to be complete, to be whole, and to finally be *enough*. To be this way in an unsafe world is to become like priests bravely setting communion tables in the presence of our enemies.

Novelist Ursula K. Le Guin once famously said, "We live in capitalism. Its power seems inescapable—but then, so did the divine right of kings. Any human power can be resisted and changed by human beings." If we will allow it, radical okayness will unlock our capacity for creative and collective resistance by introducing us to a God who self-disinterestedly loves us independently of what we do for this God's glory and bottom line. This God loves us for the same reason millions of fireflies synchronously mate in an empty field in early June— not because it is necessarily useful or productive, but because the weird, complicated, and beautiful parts of life mirror the complicated weirdness and beauty of the God who created it, and me, and you. The steady delivery of nonanxious, nontransactional love and trustworthiness in the face of profound pain is the hallmark of what it means to be part of *this* healthy family and to be raised by *this* divine parent.

Divinely ordained, radical okayness provides a fuller picture into who we can be, what we can do, and how we can do it together, whenever all of us begin entering into the pain of others and enacting this kind of love for ourselves and for the world. Fred Rogers once called this work a "neighborhood expression of care," and Tricia Hersey describes it as an act of "collective care and collective rest." The best people to save us and return us to ourselves are those we know, those we live next door to, those who come through our checkout lines, those we love and who love us, and those who would bake a casserole when there's a death in our family.

When we commune with the real world buzzing synchronously around us outside our phones, even when we have every reason to doubt and defensively recoil, we become a miracle, a prayer, a flesh-and-blood benediction. We become good news. And in so doing, we remind everyone within earshot—underneath all the branding—that there is something deep inside all of us that holds us up, unconditionally loves us, and helps us to become not who we *should* be but who we *are* for ourselves and for the world.

I still believe we might call this kind of posture "Christian," but only if we mean it as a posture of humility in the face of a universe without end. American Christianity doesn't have to remain an airless and deadening form of anxious white ownership parading as a religion. Amid bottomless capitalist exploitation, alienation, and buried pain, Christianity, in its truest form, is the cultivation of eyes, ears, hearts, and hands that remain stubbornly open to the rhythms of sacredness quietly playing underneath the anxious noise of existence. It is the practice of militant hope in the face of tired cynicism, steadfast love in the face of polarizing and crippling fear, and open-handed trust in the face of endless attempts at myopic control. It bares its scars and suddenly enters into rooms where the door is still locked. It rests. It trusts. It loves. It dies, and it rises, over and over and over again.

Becoming born again is an invitation to enter into this very same rhythm: to rest, to trust, to love, to eat bread, to drink wine, to die, and to rise again into a world where grace and peace stubbornly flicker around all of us. We don't own grace and peace, but we get them anyway. That's what makes all this good news. That's what makes it love. That's what makes it buoyant.

I hope one day we'll see this good news, hear it, and maybe even become it. But until that day comes, may you, in all your cellular complexity, be made whole not by more work or more search engine optimization but by a God of bottomless mystery willing to hold you up, look you in the eye, ask you your name, and return you to the truth of who you've always been: a human, not a brand or a bad investment. And upon finding yourself clothed and in your right mind once again, may you begin resisting the scarcity and self-interest that raised you by choosing to repair the world around you with the very same kind of radical, unconquerable, and resurrecting okayness you've received from the God at the bottom of the slippery slope.

Because when we can become restfully, radically okay together, even amid rampant pain and well-organized alienation, who knows what we could do next?

Acknowledgments

When I was in middle school, I was taught the cautionary tale of MC Hammer. Maybe you know this one—about how a man worth $70 million went bankrupt because he spent exorbitant amounts of money on sports cars, private planes, helicopters, horses, gold statues of himself, and a pool shaped like his patented baggy pants. What *VH1's Behind the Music* left out was that at the height of Hammer's career, he was employing an entourage of more than two hundred people, most of whom were out-of-work friends and family members from his old Oakland neighborhood. Hammer was a job creator who never forgot where he came from or whom he belonged to.

This book (*probably*) won't make $70 million, but it is still the product of a network of family, friends, classmates, neighbors, students, and old coworkers at the Trader Joe's on Kingston Pike. The Bible calls this kind of entourage a cloud of witnesses. I would gladly go bankrupt employing them.

To my incredibly gracious editor, Valerie Weaver-Zercher, and the whole team at Broadleaf Books: I still have no idea why you kept saying yes. To the Bobcats for teaching me how to be *real*. To friends who kept asking good questions even when I talked much too long about answers that never quite answered anything. To Justin Phillips for helping me not embarrass myself no matter how many drafts it took. To Brent Newberry for bringing me to tears at just the right time. To Rose Lee-Norman for definitely-not-enervating feedback, you were totally right. To Ken and Kim Brown, your generosity is legendary. Most of chapter 6 was written in my boxer shorts on your back porch before I locked myself out and broke into your cabin with an ax and spent the rest of the day repairing your back door. *Best distraction ever.*

To family, who gave insight, support, food, childcare, legitimate (or at least well-faked) interest, and even entire houses over the past year and a half. To John and Rachel: It meant so much to sit in your dad's den for weekend after weekend. I wish he could have talked with me about grace one more time. To Grady, for showing me what self-disinterested love looks like in a cardigan and corduroy pants. I hope one day to be as kind, humble, and consistent as you have been to your family and to your grandson-in-law. To the Howells for hanging in there while I tried to find my groove. I like who we are now. To the Renfros, for loving me like a son since I was seventeen. To Mimi and Ruby for keeping me afloat. I miss drinking Diet Dr. Pepper with you in the kitchen.

And finally, to the home team: Lindsay and Finn. While I'm still not entirely sure any of this was worth being away from you two, none of this happens without you. To Lindsay, thanks for reading along with me for the past fifteen years, encouraging me to keep going, and asking hard questions even though I get defensive and (eventually) agree with you. You save me. You love me. You believe in me. And you resurrect me over and over and over again. And to my boy: I gotta say, I haven't always loved being a Minton—that is, until you and your mom taught me what being a Minton can mean when you have enough imagination. I can't ever thank you enough for showing me how to become born again. Now enough of this; let's go ride bikes.

Notes

Chapter 1

3 **"In a study from the year 2000":** "Studies Show Normal Children Today Report More Anxiety Than Child Psychiatric Patients in the 1950s," American Psychological Association, 2000, https://www.apa.org/news/press/releases/2000/12/anxiety.

4 **"The National Institutes of Health recently reported":** Kathleen Ries Merikangas et al., "Lifetime Prevalence of Mental Disorders in U.S. Adolescents," *Journal of the American Academy of Child Adolescent Psychiatry* 49, no. 10 (October 2010): 980–89, http://www.ncbi.nlm.nih.gov/pubmed/20855043/; Sally C. Curtin and Melonie Heron, "Death Rates Due to Suicide and Homicide among Persons Aged 10–24: United States, 2000–2017," NCH Data Brief no. 352, October 2019, https://www.cdc.gov/nchs/data/databriefs/db352-h.pdf.

6 **"Most of us were not taught":** Brené Brown, *Braving the Wilderness: The Quest for True Belonging and the Courage to Stand Alone* (New York: Random House, 2017), 84.

7 **"Malcolm Harris aptly describes":** Malcolm Harris, *Kids These Days: Human Capital and the Making of Millennials* (New York: Little, Brown, 2017), 35.

8 **"This kind of life":** Niraj Chokshi, "Americans Are among the Most Stressed People in the World, Poll Finds," *New York Times*, April 25, 2019, https://www.nytimes.com/2019/04/25/us/americans-stressful.html.

8 **"Depression embodies the final dissent of soul":** Bruce Rogers-Vaughn, "Blessed Are Those Who Mourn: Depression as Political Resistance," *Pastoral Psychology* 63 (2014): 515.

8 **"In *Remember This House*":** Raoul Peck, dir., *I Am Not Your Negro* (New York: Magnolia Pictures, 2016).

Chapter 2

12 **"All of a sudden":** Benoit Denizet-Lewis, "Why Are More American Teenagers Than Ever Suffering from Severe Anxiety?," *New York Times*, October 11, 2017, https://tinyurl.com/a5b9eh3j.

13 **"For Jake":** Denizet-Lewis.

13 **"Three years later"**: Jason Plautz, "The Environmental Burden of Generation Z," *Washington Post*, February 3, 2020, https://www.washingtonpost.com/magazine/2020/02/03/eco-anxiety-is-overwhelming-kids-wheres-line-between-education-alarmism/?arc404=true.

15 **"Glennon Doyle perfectly encapsulates"**: Glennon Doyle, *Untamed* (New York: Dial, 2020), 155.

15 **"Despite how all this anxiety"**: Juliana Menasce Horowitz and Nikki Graf, "Most U.S. Teens See Anxiety and Depression as a Major Problem among Their Peers," Pew Research Center, February 20, 2019, https://www.pewsocialtrends.org/2019/02/20/most-u-s-teens-see-anxiety-and-depression-as-a-major-problem-among-their-peers/.

15 **"When these findings"**: "Children's Hospitals Admissions for Suicidal Thoughts, Actions Double during Past Decade," AAP News, May 4, 2017, https://www.aappublications.org/news/2017/05/04/PASSuicide050417.

17 **"Maybe our kids"**: Harris, *Kids These Days*, 7.

17 **"In his book *Strangers to Ourselves*"**: Timothy D. Wilson, *Strangers to Ourselves: Discovering the Adaptive Unconscious* (Cambridge, MA: Harvard University Press, 2004), 24.

17 **"Wilson quips that"**: Wilson, 6.

18 **"It can thus be fruitless"**: Wilson, 16.

18 **"Or why has popular educational policy"**: Daphne Bassok, Scott Latham, and Anna Rorem, "Is Kindergarten the New First Grade?," *AERA Open* 1, no. 4 (2016): 1–31, https://journals.sagepub.com/doi/pdf/10.1177/2332858415616358.

19 **"In 2015, the USDA"**: "The Cost of Raising a Child," USDA, February 18, 2020, https://www.usda.gov/media/blog/2017/01/13/cost-raising-child.

19 **"Emory University sociologist"**: Sabino Kornrich, "Inequalities in Parental Spending on Young Children: 1972–2010," *AERA Open* 2, no. 2 (2016): 1–12, https://journals.sagepub.com/doi/pdf/10.1177/2332858416644180.

20 **"Without succumbing to political nightmares"**: Robert D. Putnam, *Our Kids: The American Dream in Crisis* (New York: Simon & Schuster, 2015), 240.

20 **"A 2017 *Time* cover story"**: Sean Gregory, "How Kids' Sports Became a $15 Billion Industry," *Time*, August 24, 2017, https://time.com/magazine/us/4913681/september-4th-2017-vol-190-no-9-u-s/.

21 **"In 2018, the *Atlantic* found"**: Derek Thompson, "American Meritocracy Is Killing Youth Sports," *Atlantic*, November 6, 2018, https://www.theatlantic.com/ideas/archive/2018/11/income-inequality-explains-decline-youth-sports/574975/.

21 **"In this kind of environment"**: Harris, *Kids These Days*, 11.

21 **"Sports psychologist Jim Taylor"**: Gregory, "How Kids' Sports."

22 **"A 2016 study"**: Charles R. Dunn et al., "The Impact of Family Financial Investment on Perceived Pressure and Child Enjoyment and Commitment in Organized Youth Sport," *Journal of Family Relations* 65, no. 2 (2016): 287–99.

22 **"Just like you needn't be"**: Sandra Hofferth, "Changes in American Children's Time—1997 to 2003," *Electronic International Journal of Time Use Research* 6, no. 1 (2009): 26–47, https://doi.org/10.13085/eIJTUR.6.1.26-47.

23 **"American Millennials Are among"**: Anne Fisher, "American Millennials Are among the World's Least Skilled," *Fortune*, March 10, 2015, https://fortune.com/2015/03/10/american-millennials-are-among-the-worlds-least-skilled/.

23 **"How the Baby Boomers"**: Sean Illing, "How the Baby Boomers—Not Millennials—Screwed America," *Vox*, October 26, 2019, https://www.vox.com/2017/12/20/16772670/baby-boomers-millennials-congress-debt.

24 **"Journalist Anne Helen Petersen"**: Anne Helen Petersen, *Can't Even: How Millennials Became the Burnout Generation* (New York: Mariner Books, 2020), xix.

24 **"Once again, Malcolm Harris"**: Harris, *Kids These Days*, 4.

24 **"As sociologist Tressie McMillan Cottom"**: Tressie McMillan Cottom, "Nearly Six Decades after the Civil Rights Movement, Why Do Black Workers Still Have to Hustle to Get Ahead?," *Time*, February 20, 2020.

25 **"And why we report"**: Brian Resnick, "22 Percent of Millennials Say They Have 'No Friends,'" *Vox*, August 1, 2019, https://www.vox.com/science-and-health/2019/8/1/20750047/millennials-poll-loneliness.

25 **"Most of us would rather"**: Petersen, *Can't Even*, xx.

Chapter 3

29 **"When we bring our wits"**: David Dark, *Everyday Apocalypse* (Grand Rapids, MI: Baker Books, 2002), 15.

30 **"If you're going to spend"**: Holly Ellyatt, "How I Helped Get Trump Elected: The President's Digital Guru," CNBC, November 8, 2017, https://www.cnbc.com/2017/11/08/how-i-helped-get-trump-elected-the-presidents-digital-guru-brad-parscale.html.

30 **"David Dark refers"**: David Dark, *Life's Too Short to Pretend You Aren't Religious* (Downers Grove, IL: IVP, 2016), 103.

30 **"In 2005, roughly 5 percent"**: "Social Media Fact Sheet," Pew Research Group, April 7, 2020, https://www.pewresearch.org/internet/fact-sheet/social-media/.

30 **"The average length of time"**: H. Tankovska, "Daily Time Spent on Social Networking by Internet Users Worldwide from 2012–2020," Statista, June 30, 2021, https://www.statista.com/statistics/433871/daily-social-media-usage-worldwide/.

31 **"After digging into the raw"**: Adam Alter, *Irresistible: The Rise of Addictive Technology and the Business of Keeping Us Hooked* (New York: Penguin, 2017), 15.

31 **"Lanier refers to"**: Jaron Lanier, *You Are Not a Gadget* (New York: Knopf, 2010), 39.

32 **"To better understand"**: Agam Bansal et al., "Selfies: A Boon or Bane?," *Journal of Family Medicine and Primary Care* 7, no. 4 (July–August 2018): 828–31, https://www.ncbi.nlm.nih.gov/pmc/articles/PMC6131996/.

33 **"Here's Lanier again"**: Lanier, *You Are Not a Gadget*, 53.

33 **"Historian Yuval Noah Harari"**: Yuval Noah Harari, "Why Technology Favors Tyranny," *Atlantic*, October 2018, https://www.theatlantic.com/magazine/archive/2018/10/yuval-noah-harari-technology-tyranny/568330/.

35 **"I suppose that when"**: Jon Ronson, *So You've Been Publicly Shamed* (New York: Riverhead, 2015), 56.

35 **"In every compassionate"**: Ronson, 310.

36 **"One of the most destructive"**: Jaron Lanier, *Ten Reasons You Should Delete Your Social Media Account Right Now* (New York: Henry Holt, 2018), 20.

36 **"This leaves Lanier to gloomily"**: Noah Kulwin, "'One Has This Feeling of Having Contributed to Something That's Gone Very Wrong,'" *New York Magazine*, April 2018, https://nymag.com/intelligencer/2018/04/jaron-lanier-interview-on-what-went-wrong-with-the-internet.html.

37 **"Alter notes"**: Alter, *Irresistible*, 40.

Chapter 4

41 **"When I was three"**: Jane Anderson, "The Impact of Family Structure on the Health of Children: Effects of Divorce," *Linacre Quarterly* 81, no. 4 (November 2014): 378–87, https://doi.org/10.1179/0024363914Z.00000000087.

44 **"In the day-to-day trenches"**: David Foster Wallace, *This Is Water: Some Thoughts, Delivered on a Significant Occasion about Living a Compassionate Life* (New York: Little, Brown, 2009), 98–113, 132–33.

45 **"In his landmark book"**: Walter Wink, *The Powers That Be: Theology for a New Millennium* (New York: Harmony, 1999), 2.

46 **"Over the past thirty years"**: Mark Fisher, *Capitalist Realism: Is There No Alternative?* (London: Zero, 2009), 16–17.

46 **"Capitalism provides the"**: Ibram X. Kendi, *How to Be an Antiracist* (New York: One World, 2019), 163.

47 **"This logic was employed in direct"**: Doha Madani, "Dan Patrick on Coronavirus: 'More Important Things Than Living,'" NBC News, April 21, 2020, https://www.nbcnews.com/news/us-news/texas-lt-gov-dan-patrick-reopening-economy-more-important-things-n1188911.

48 **"In his book *This City Is Killing Me*"**: Jonathan Foiles, *This City Is Killing Me: Community Trauma and Toxic Stress in Urban America* (Cleveland, OH: Belt, 2019), 18.

49 **"He notes"**: Fisher, *Capitalist Realism*, 19.

49 **"These findings lead Rogers-Vaughn"**: Bruce Rogers-Vaughn, *Caring for Souls in a Neoliberal Age* (New York: Palgrave Macmillan, 2016), 58–61.

50 **"In a 2019 paper"**: Kristen L. Syme and Edward H. Hagen, "Mental Health Is Biological Health: Why Tackling 'Diseases of the Mind' Is an Imperative for Biological

Anthropology in the 21st Century," *American Journal of Physical Anthropology* 171 (2020): 87–117, https://onlinelibrary.wiley.com/doi/full/10.1002/ajpa.23965.

51 **"Historian Eugene McCarraher":** Eugene McCarraher, *The Enchantment of Mammon: How Capitalism Became the Religion of Modernity* (Cambridge, MA: Belknap, 2019), 581.

51 **"Under capitalism":** McCarraher, 9–11 (commentary note is mine).

52 **"Almost 67 percent of American bankruptcies":** Bob Herman, "Health Care CEO Pay Tops $1 Billion in 2018 So Far," *Axios*, April 8, 2019, https://www.axios.com/health-care-ceo-salaries-2018-3aff66cd-8723-4ec8-abe8-dd19edd24390.html?utm_source=twitter&utm_medium=social&utm_campaign=organic.

54 **"Sermonizing for his parishioners":** Victor Garcia, "Hannity Slams 'Bolshevik' Bernie Sanders, Says Socialism Results in 'Nothing but Suffering and Carnage,'" Fox News, February 24, 2020, https://www.foxnews.com/media/hannity-slams-bernie-sanders-and-socialism.

55 **"In his book *The Market as God*":** Harvey Cox, *The Market as God* (Cambridge, MA: Harvard University Press, 2016), 6.

55 **"This impulse may explain":** "$1.6B of Bank Bailout Went to Execs," AP News, December 21, 2008, https://www.cbsnews.com/news/16b-of-bank-bailout-went-to-execs/.

56 **"Research is now showing":** Scott Simon, Josh Axelrod, and Samantha Balaban, "Isolated and Struggling, Many Seniors Are Turning to Suicide," NPR, July 27, 2019, https://www.npr.org/2019/07/27/745017374/isolated-and-struggling-many-seniors-are-turning-to-suicide.

56 **"We just need more patience":** Yuval Noah Harari, *Sapiens: A Brief History of Humankind* (New York: Harper, 2015), 333.

57 **"'cult of minimal variation'":** Fisher, *Capitalist Realism*, 76.

Chapter 5

61 **"Ibram X. Kendi deftly defines":** Kendi, *How to Be an Antiracist*, 169.

62 **"White self-sufficient masculinity":** Willie James Jennings, *After Whiteness: An Education in Belonging* (Grand Rapids, MI: Eerdmans, 2020), 8–9.

63 **"I don't remember anyone":** "Short-Term Mission Trips: Are They Worth the Investment?," Baylor University Media and Public Relations, May 2, 2011, https://www.baylor.edu/mediacommunications/news.php?action=story&story=93238.

65 **"Despite the very real contextual differences":** Francis FitzGerald, *The Evangelicals: The Struggle to Shape America* (New York: Simon & Schuster, 2017), 3.

66 **"Interestingly, FitzGerald understands":** FitzGerald, 4.

66 **"Kruse summarizes the aims":** Kevin Kruse, *One Nation under God: How Corporate America Invented Christian America* (New York: Basic, 2016), 7.

67 **"[Graham] spoke at length":** Kruse, 51.

68 **"Writing all the way back in 1929":** Richard H. Niebuhr, *The Social Sources of Denominationalism* (Gloucester, MA: Peter Smith, 1929), 30–31.

68 **"For the churches of the Middle Class":** Niebuhr, 85–86.

68 **"Two decades earlier":** Max Weber, *The Protestant Ethic and Spirit of Capitalism* (New York: Scribner, 1958), 66.

69 **"Typically, we will see":** Soong Chan-Rah, *The Next Evangelicalism: Freeing the Church from Western Cultural Captivity* (Westmont, IL: IVP, 2009), 56.

69 **"Instead of offering":** Karl Marx, *Critique of Hegel's "Philosophy of Right,"* ed. Joseph O'Malley, trans. Annette Jolin and Joseph O'Malley (New York: Cambridge University Press, 1970).

72 **"These beliefs include":** Christian Smith and Melinda Lundquist Denton, *Soul Searching: The Religious and Spiritual Lives of American Teenagers* (Oxford: Oxford University Press, 2005), 162–63.

73 **"In interviews with teenagers":** Christian Smith, "On 'Moralistic Therapeutic Deism' as U.S. Teenagers' Actual, Tacit, De Facto Religious Faith," in *The 2005 Princeton Lectures on Youth, Church, and Culture: With Energy, Intelligence, Imagination, and Love: Leadership in Youth Ministry,* ed. Amy Scott Vaughn (Princeton, NJ: Princeton Theological Seminary, 2005), 46–57.

73 **"Moralistic Therapeutic Deism":** Smith and Denton, *Soul Searching,* 169.

74 **"Smith and Denton conclude as much":** Smith and Denton, 170.

76 **"At church camp youth group":** Grace Semler Baldridge, "Youth Group," track 5 on *Preacher's Kid,* self-recorded, 2021. Included with artist permission.

Chapter 6

78 **"Buddhist mystic and psychotherapist John Welwood":** Tina Fossella, "Human Nature, Buddha Nature: An Interview with John Welwood," *Tricycle: The Buddhist Review* 20, no. 3 (Spring 2011): 1–18.

79 **"The study found that pastors'":** "Clergy More Likely to Suffer from Depression, Anxiety," *Duke Today,* August 27, 2013, https://today.duke.edu/2013/08/clergydepressionnewsrelease.

80 **"She found that":** Anne Helen Petersen, "The Contours of Clergy Burnout," *Culture Study,* September 24, 2020, https://annehelen.substack.com/p/the-contours-of-clergy-burnout.

80 **"Nothing that has happened to me since":** James Baldwin, "Down at the Cross," in *Collected Essays,* ed. Toni Morrison (New York: Library of America, 1998), 306.

83 **"The American Negro":** Baldwin, 344.

84 **"These many forms":** Ibram X. Kendi, *Stamped from the Beginning: The Definitive History of Racist Ideas in America* (New York: Nation Books, 2016), 506.

86   **"And right there":** Lawrence Kushner, *Eyes Remade for Wonder: A Lawrence Kushner Reader* (Woodstock, VT: Jewish Lights, 1998), 176.

89   **"He suggests that":** Richard Kearney, *Anatheism: Returning to God after God* (New York: Columbia University Press, 2010), 185.

Chapter 7

94   **"A symmetry can be seen":** René Girard, *The Scapegoat* (Baltimore: Johns Hopkins University Press, 1986), 171.

95   **"'Lying flat' (or *tangping* in Mandarin)":** Elsie Chen, "These Chinese Millennials Are Chilling and Beijing Isn't Happy," *New York Times*, July 3, 2021, https://tinyurl .com/3akrs8rb.

98   **"Or as Adichie's protagonist":** Chimamanda Ngozi Adichie, *Americanah* (New York: Knopf, 2013), 359.

99   **"Caruso argues":** Julie Beck, "How to Get Better at Expressing Emotions," *Atlantic*, November 18, 2015, https://www.theatlantic.com/health/archive/2015/11/how-to -get-better-at-expressing-emotions/416493/.

99   **"University of Toronto psychologist Brett Ford":** Brett Ford et al., "The Psychological Health Benefits of Accepting Negative Emotions and Thoughts: Laboratory, Diary, and Longitudinal Evidence," *Journal of Personality and Social Psychology* 115, no. 6 (December 2018): 1075–92, https://pubmed.ncbi.nlm.nih.gov/28703602/.

99   **"Over time, Ford notes that these feelings":** Allyson Chiu, "Time to Ditch 'Toxic Positivity,' Experts Say: 'It's Okay Not to Be Okay,'" *Washington Post*, August 19, 2020, https://www.washingtonpost.com/lifestyle/wellness/toxic-positivity-mental -health-covid/2020/08/19/5dff8d16-e0c8-11ea-8181-606e603bb1c4_story.html.

102 **"Frustratingly, whenever these expressed feelings":** Rogers-Vaughn, "Blessed," 515.

103 **"In this kind of system":** Wink, *Powers That Be*, 2.

103 **"Theologian and professor of philosophy Cornel West":** Cornel West, *Democracy Matters: Winning the Fight against Imperialism* (New York: Penguin, 2004), 27.

105 **"But if we have ears to hear":** Bruce Rogers-Vaughn, "Recovering Grief in the Age of Recovery," *Journal of Pastoral Theology* 13, no. 1 (June 2003): 42.

107 **"Here's how Brené Brown describes":** Brown, *Braving the Wilderness*, 85.

109 **"I think what":** David Remnick, "Chance the Rapper's Art and Activism," July 20, 2020, in *New Yorker: Politics and More*, podcast, 21:53, https://www.newyorker .com/podcast/political-scene/chance-the-rappers-art-and-activism.

110 **"When we look down through":** West, *Democracy Matters*, 20.

111 **"In *The Fire Next Time*":** James Baldwin, "My Dungeon Shook," in Morrison, *Collected Essays*, 294.

Chapter 8

114 **"Du Mez describes":** Kristin Kobes Du Mez, *Jesus and John Wayne: How White Evangelicals Corrupted a Faith and Fractured a Nation* (New York: Liveright, 2020), 295.

114 **"Caught up in authoritarian settings":** Du Mez, 278.

116 **"Writing for the *New York Times*":** Jonathan Merritt, "It's Getting Harder to Talk about God," *New York Times*, October 13, 2018, https://www.nytimes.com/2018/10/13/opinion/sunday/talk-god-sprituality-christian.html.

116 **"Many people now avoid":** Merritt.

117 **"Evangelicals hadn't betrayed":** Du Mez, *Jesus and John Wayne*, 271.

119 **"In short, the aim of":** Terry and Sharon Hargraves, "Restoring Identity," *Fuller Magazine*, no. 6 (2018), https://www.fuller.edu/wp-content/uploads/2018/03/Restoring-Identity_Hargraves_FullerSeminary.pdf.

120 **"When I once described":** Story included with patient permission.

121 **"In one interview":** "From Here to Eternity," *Psychology Today*, March 1993, https://www.psychologytoday.com/us/articles/199303/here-eternity.

123 **"Anne Helen Petersen defines":** Petersen, *Can't Even*, 209.

123 **"Glennon Doyle lays bare":** Doyle, *Untamed*, 75.

126 **"Over a long enough time":** Ivan Boszormenyi-Nagy and Geraldine Spark, *Invisible Loyalties: Reciprocity in Intergenerational Family Therapy* (New York: Brunner/Mazel, 1984), 152.

128 **"Williams argues":** Delores S. Williams, *Sisters in the Wilderness: The Challenge of Womanist God-Talk* (New York: Orbis, 1993), 5.

Chapter 9

134 **"In May 2018, the *Chicago Tribune*":** Kate Thayer, "Youth Sports Faces Shortage of Refs Who 'Don't Want to Stand There and Take the Abuse,'" *Chicago Tribune*, May 2, 2018, https://www.chicagotribune.com/lifestyles/ct-life-youth-sports-ref-shortage-20180501-story.html.

134 **"Adults want to win":** Thayer.

135 **"This, for Petersen":** Petersen, *Can't Even*, 51–53.

137 **"What is 'heaven'":** Bright Eyes, "Land Locked Blues," track 8 on *I'm Wide Awake, It's Morning*, Saddle Creek Records, 2005.

137 **"In his book *My Bright Abyss*":** Christian Wiman, *My Bright Abyss: Meditation of a Modern Believer* (New York: Farrar, Straus & Giroux, 2013), 167.

138 **"Sometimes God calls":** Wiman, 61.

142 **"How are we to proclaim the God":** Gustavo Gutiérrez, *On Job: God Talk and the Suffering of the Innocent* (Maryknoll, NY: Orbis, 1987), xiv–xvii.

143 **"It is a posture expressly rejecting":** Gutiérrez, 1.

144 **"From the philosophical ruminations"**: Samuel Balentine, *Job*, Smyth & Helwys Bible Commentary 10 (Macon, GA: Smith & Helwys, 2006), 4.

147 **"As Gutiérrez argues"**: Gutiérrez, *On Job*, 13.

149 **"In one sense"**: Kelefa Sanneh, "The Hell Raiser," *New Yorker*, November 26, 2012, https://www.newyorker.com/magazine/2012/11/26/the-hell-raiser-3.

151 **"But instead of using it"**: "Mellody's Math: Delivered from Debt," ABC News, January 6, 2006, https://abcnews.go.com/GMA/story?id=125995&page=1.

151 **"With Ephesus down"**: Anne Helen Petersen, "This Sort-of Socialist Church Is Taking a Radical Approach to Christianity," Buzzfeed News, December 12, 2019, https://www.buzzfeednews.com/article/annehelenpetersen/jubilee-baptist-church-debt-forgiveness-lgbtq-socialism.

152 **"There are these kids"**: Petersen.

152 **"Richard Rohr once"**: Richard Rohr, *Everything Belongs: The Gift of Contemplative Prayer* (Chestnut Ridge, NY: Crossroad, 2003), 128.

Chapter 10

160 **"You know, when"**: Dylan Marron, "Empathy Is Not Endorsement," *TED2018*, April 2018, https://www.ted.com/talks/dylan_marron_empathy_is_not_endorsement.

162 **"These partisan megaidentities"**: Ezra Klein, *Why We're Polarized* (New York: Avid Reader, 2020), 68–74.

162 **"I imagine one"**: James Baldwin, "Me and My House," *Harper's Magazine*, November 1955, 54–61.

163 **"She argues that"**: Rebecca Solnit, "On Not Meeting Nazis Halfway," *Literary Hub*, November 19, 2020, https://lithub.com/rebecca-solnit-on-not-meeting-nazis-halfway/.

164 **"Boszormenyi-Nagy and Krasner argue"**: Ivan Boszormenyi-Nagy and Barbara Krasner, *Between Give and Take: A Clinical Guide to Contextual Therapy* (New York: Brunner/Mazel, 1986), 302.

164 **"People take time"**: Dark, *Life's Too Short*, 113.

165 **"I think we overuse"**: Jessica Bennett, "What If Instead of Calling People Out, We Called Them In?," *New York Times*, November 19, 2020, https://tinyurl.com/2x7vpt9y.

169 **"A few towns over"**: D. Bratcher, *The Enuma Elish: The Babylonian Creation Myth* (n.p.: CRI/Voice, 2018), https://www.crivoice.org/enumaelish.html.

Chapter 11

176 **"What is grace?"**: Tom Junod, "Can You Say . . . Hero?," *Esquire*, November 1998, https://www.esquire.com/entertainment/tv/a27134/can-you-say-hero-esq1198/.

177 **"Pain is unrelenting"**: Brown, *Braving the Wilderness*, 84.

179 **"He says"**: Abraham Joshua Heschel, *The Sabbath: Its Meaning for Modern Man* (New York: FSG, 1951), ix.

180 **"When Black and brown labor"**: Tricia Hersey, the Nap Ministry, https://thenapministry.wordpress.com.

180 **"Caring for myself"**: Audre Lorde, *A Burst of Light and Other Essays* (Mineola, NY: Ixia, 2017), 130.

184 **"Novelist Ursula K. Le Guin"**: "The National Book Foundation Medal for Distinguished Contribution to American Letters Acceptance Speech," Ursulakleguin.com, November 25, 2011, https://www.ursulakleguin.com/nbf-medal.

185 **"expression of care"**: "May 1, 1969: Fred Rogers testifies before the Senate Subcommittee on Communications," video, 6:50, February 8, 2015, https://www.youtube.com/watch?v=fKy7ljRr0AA.

185 **"collective rest"**: Tricia Hersey, "Slowly Emerging After a 3 Week Sabbath," *The Nap Ministry* (blog), July 14, 2020, https://www.thenapministry.wordpress.com.